Arrival Stories

Arrival Stories

WOMEN SHARE THEIR EXPERIENCES OF BECOMING MOTHERS

Collected by Amy Schumer
and Christy Turlington Burns

RANDOM HOUSE
LARGE PRINT

Published in the United States of America by
Random House Large Print in association with The Dial Press,
an imprint of Random House, a division of
Penguin Random House LLC, New York.

Contributor credits are on pages 249–250.
Photo credits are on page 251.

Cover design: Donna Cheng
Cover illustration: Kenesha Sneed

The Library of Congress has established a
Cataloging-in-Publication record for this title.

ISBN: 978-0-593-40142-2

www.penguinrandomhouse.com/large-print-format-books

FIRST LARGE PRINT EDITION

Printed in the United States of America

1st Printing

This Large Print edition published in accord with
the standards of the N.A.V.H.

To the women who tell their stories
To everyone who listens
To every mother, everywhere

Stories matter. Many stories matter. Stories have been used to dispossess and to malign, but stories can also be used to empower and to humanize. Stories can break the dignity of a people, but stories can also repair that broken dignity.

—CHIMAMANDA NGOZI ADICHIE

Contents

Introduction

It's time to break one of the unspoken rules of motherhood. Since, well, **forever,** women have been taught not to tell the story of birthing our babies. Taught by whom? Well, that's a story for a whole other book but, unbelievably, in the year 2022, it feels like the rule still applies. What happens to us in the most vulnerable and powerful hours of our lives isn't supposed to be shared in all its stark, bloody detail. Instead, we are told to be grateful, to accept pain and suffering as simply part of the gig of motherhood. Conception, pregnancy, birth, matching with your baby through adoption, or the period of time after birth can be incredibly difficult, frightening, even traumatic. It can also be joyful and empowering. And it can be all these things at the same time. No matter how it happens, the arrival of a child is a life-altering event. And yet, all too often we keep quiet about our experiences. Why shouldn't we talk about the beautiful mess of it all?

Change often begins with the simple act of people coming together to share knowledge and experience to lift each other up. This is how we birth ideas and cultural movements: together. Life is about sharing stories. These are some **Arrival Stories.** This book was born in conversation between Amy Schumer and Christy Turlington Burns when Amy was very pregnant and Christy visited her. After months of throwing up every single day, Amy had been diagnosed with hyperemesis gravidarum, an extreme form of morning sickness. When she shared the story of her illness—the raw, unvarnished truth of it—on social media, friends and strangers alike responded with incredible messages of support. Amy went from feeling isolated in her struggle, to understanding that many others had persevered through the same or similar challenges. Hearing their stories gave Amy the comradery and the encouragement she desperately needed at that time. But Amy soon saw that it didn't end with her. When she heard from other women who saw themselves in her story, Amy realized that sharing had not only helped her, it had helped other people too.

Amy wanted to find a way to keep the chain going, to pay her good fortune forward. Talking to Christy, she learned more about Christy's nonprofit organization, Every Mother Counts, which seeks to make pregnancy and birth safe for women all over the globe. Christy started Every Mother Counts in 2010, after suffering from a retained placenta and severe bleeding hours after delivering her healthy daughter. Christy sensed that Amy was ready to handle the devastating truth of maternal healthcare and so she decided to share the statistics.

In the United States, maternal healthcare is in crisis. Our country has the highest maternal mortality rate in the developed world. Although most are preventable, maternal deaths have been increasing in the U.S. since 2000. It's worse for women of color, who are three times more likely to die than their white counterparts. Even in a wealthy city like New York (where Amy was born), women of color are **twelve times** more likely to die unnecessarily from childbirth. These statistics rocked Amy to her core. It all begged the question, one that Christy has been asking since she started Every Mother Counts more than a decade ago: **Why** are so many mothers dying?

Women, especially women of color, do not have a voice in a biased system that has long been much more invested in the research and funding of men's health issues. In 2020, a United Nations global report found that close to 90 percent of all people are biased against women, and the medical world is no exception. Medical research has often excluded women, partially because scientists wrongfully assumed that their hormones and menstrual cycles made them difficult to study. A 2018 study found that doctors often view men with chronic pain as "brave" or "stoic," but they described women with chronic pain as "emotional" or "hysterical." The U.S. also has a history of denying Black women their consent for performing medical experiments. Looking at the systemic racism embedded in every American institution, it's not surprising to find it deeply entrenched in the medical world. But that doesn't mean we must accept a high maternal mortality rate as a permanent reality of living in America. We must not let racism, sexism, or any other scourge of humankind keep women unsafe. Every mother deserves safety and protection not only for her baby but for herself too.

After Amy talked to Christy, she couldn't stop thinking about the indelible crash course in maternal health she'd been given. Soon enough, she called Christy with the idea to curate a collection of birth stories from many kinds of mothers, a book that would push back against the mandate to stay silent about our experiences, against the implicit notion that our pain is not important. The book would be a way to extend a hand to women everywhere, to say: **I want to hear your story. And here's mine, here's hers, and here are others'. You are not alone. How can we help each other?** Christy was, of course, enthralled with the idea. And so the two set about making a list of some of the most dynamic mothers they knew.

Arrival Stories is a collection of more than twenty unique birth stories, but also **rebirth** stories. **Our** rebirths. A woman is reborn when she leaps from the edge of who she once was into the fire of a new identity: mother. Transformation doesn't just happen with the arrival of one's first child. Whether it's the first time a woman welcomes a child into the world, or the fifth, each birth experience is life-changing, each time is singular. And transformation pours out beyond labor, beyond the operating room or the home birthing pool. The title **Arrival Stories** comes from the idea that arriving at motherhood, or parenthood, is a process, and it can happen at any time: the first time the baby kicks in utero, in the middle of the night while nursing or bottle-feeding, or while you're crying from gratitude and exhaustion at your baby's first birthday party, or maybe you don't feel you've "arrived" at motherhood until you're in a therapy session three years after your child's birth. There are many moments of arrival to motherhood, and once there, the experience keeps deepening, even after your "baby" is all grown up.

Between the covers of this book, you will meet all kinds of women—doctors, daughters, sisters, writers, wives, academics, comedians, doulas, actors, athletes, models, executives—at their most primal, and their most resourceful. In no way do these stories represent the whole spectrum of birthing experiences. While the contributors in this collection identify as women, we understand that gender is not binary and that there are millions of people who do not identify as women who have arrival stories to share. This book is meant to be a conversation starter, and we encourage people who do not see themselves represented in these pages to share their stories, to let their experiences be known. We want to hear more; we will never stop listening.

We told our stories too. Even though it's been eighteen years since Christy gave birth to her daughter, Grace, telling the story of Grace's birth here allowed Christy the opportunity to see it in a new way, informed as she is now by the years of work she has done with Every Mother Counts. Not being able to birth her placenta led Christy to investigate what happens to other mothers in similar circumstances around the world, a quest that "gave birth" to Every Mother Counts. Reading the other women's stories has been profound too. There's elation, bliss, loss, and the purest sorrow on these pages. There are healing, hilarious moments, and moments that remind us of the innate wisdom of our instincts. The spectrum of the motherhood experience is on display in this collection.

This book is for everyone—all birthing people, every configuration of family, and for those who are not mothers now, and won't, can't, or don't want to be mothers in the future. We were all **born** from a mother, every single one of us, so we all benefit from knowing more about these experiences. We hope that as you read these essays, you'll see the power of sharing the unique, raw, brutal, and treasured moments that we all face in life. Telling these stories is a way of gathering our resources, our strength, and our will to fight. Our collective ferocious power will go toward changing the dangerous and unsafe conditions in maternal healthcare. Thank you for joining us in changing what we cannot accept. We are proud to do the work alongside you.

—AMY SCHUMER AND CHRISTY TURLINGTON BURNS

Fighting to Be Heard

SERENA WILLIAMS

Champion Tennis Player

My body has belonged to tennis for so long. I gripped my first racket at age three and played my first pro game at fourteen. The sport has torn me up: I've rolled my ankles, busted my knees, played with a taped-up Achilles heel, and quit mid-game from back spasms. I've suffered every injury imaginable, and I know my body.

When I found out I was pregnant two days before the 2017 Australian Open, my body had already switched allegiances. Its purpose, as far as it was concerned, was to grow and nurture this baby that had seemingly materialized, unplanned. Being pregnant wasn't something I could tell Alexis over the phone; I told him to fly out to Melbourne right away. When he got there, I handed him a paper bag filled with six positive pregnancy tests I had taken all in one afternoon.

Of course, being pregnant didn't mean I couldn't play tennis. I was scheduled to compete at eight weeks along. I wasn't sure how the Open would go; during training, I was getting more fatigued between points. Each morning—and I'm not a morning person to begin with—I was still determined to play fast and hard before the Melbourne heat socked me. I won seven matches, all in straight sets.

Since having my baby, the stakes of the game have shifted for me. I have twenty-three Grand Slams to my name, more than any other active player. But winning is now a desire and no longer a need. I have a beautiful daughter at home; I still want the titles, the success, and the esteem, but it's not my reason for waking up in the morning. There is more to teach her about this game than winning. I've learned to dust myself off after defeat, to stand up for what matters at any cost, to call out for what's fair—even when it makes me unpopular. Giving birth to my baby, it turned out, was a test for how loud and how often I would have to call out before I was finally heard.

Let's go back to the beginning. My first trimester brought headaches and a weird metallic taste in my mouth, but all in all, I had a wonderful pregnancy. I guess I'm one of those women who like being pregnant; I enjoyed the positive attention. I'm used to getting negative attention from the press and critics, but this was different. I settled into a whole new way of being. I was relaxed not playing: My life was just sitting at home, and it was wonderful. I still had plenty of work to do, but my focus narrowed to keeping myself healthy for the baby.

Don't ask me why but I was obsessed with having the baby in September, so I put off the doctors when they wanted to induce me in late August. I finally went in on August 31, and they inserted a little pill inside of me to get things going. Contractions started shortly after that and it was great! I know that's not what people are supposed to say, but I was enjoying it, the work of labor. I was completely in the moment. I loved the cramps. I loved feeling my body trying to push the baby out. I wasn't on an epidural; to get through it, I was using my breath and all the techniques I'd learned from birth training. (I had taken every birthing class that the hospital had to offer.)

By the next morning, the contractions were coming harder and faster. With each one, my baby's heart rate plummeted. I was scared. I thought I should probably get an epidural, but I was still okay with the work, so I didn't. Every time the baby's heart rate dropped, the nurses would come in and tell me to turn onto my side. The baby's heart rate would go back up and everything seemed fine. I'd have another contraction, and the baby's heart rate would drop again, but I'd turn over and the rate would go back up, and so on and so forth.

Outside of my birthing room, there were meetings going on without me—my husband was conferencing with the doctors. By this point, I was more than ready for the epidural, but after twenty minutes, the doctor walked in, looked at me and said, "We're giving you a C-section." She made it clear that there wasn't time for an epidural or more pushing. I loved her confidence; had she given me the choice between more pushing or surgery, I would have been ruined. I'm not good at making decisions. In that moment, what I needed most was that calm, affirmative direction. Since it was my first child, I really wanted to have the baby vaginally, but once the doctor made up her mind, I was on board. I thought to myself, **I've had so many surgeries, what's another one?** Being an athlete is so often about controlling your body, wielding its power, but it's also about knowing when to surrender. I was happy and relieved to let go; the energy in the room totally changed. We went from this intense, seemingly endless process to a clear plan for bringing this baby into the world.

I was nervous about meeting my baby. Throughout my pregnancy, I'd never felt a connection with her. While I loved being pregnant, I didn't have that amazing **Oh my god, this is my baby** moment, ever. It's something people don't usually talk about, because we're supposed to be in love from the first second. Yes, I was a lioness who would protect her baby at any cost, but I wasn't gushing over her. I kept waiting to feel like I **knew** her during pregnancy, but the feeling never came. Some of my mom friends told me they didn't feel the connection in the womb either, which made me feel better but, still, I longed for it.

When I finally saw her—and I just knew it was going to be a girl, that was one thing I knew about her before we even had it confirmed—I loved her right away. It wasn't exactly instantaneous, but it was there, and from that seed, it grew. I couldn't stop staring at her, my Olympia.

An hour later, they had to knock me out; I spent the night in the hospital with my baby in the room. When I woke up, she was nestled in my arms. The rest of my body was paralyzed. I couldn't get out of bed because my legs were still numb, but it didn't matter. Alexis and I sat there, alone with our new baby. It was surreal to feel the presence of this third person in the room. **Who was this new little creature?**

So much of what happened after that is still a blur. In my haze, I wondered if I should ask someone about my drip. In 2010, I learned I had blood clots in my lungs, clots that had they not been caught in time, could have killed me. Ever since then, I've lived in fear of them returning. It wasn't a one-off; I'm at high risk for blood clots. I asked a nurse, "When do I start my heparin drip? Shouldn't I be on that now?"

The response was "Well, we don't really know if that's what you need to be on right now." No one was really listening to what I was saying. The logic for not starting the blood thinners was that it could cause my C-section wound to bleed, which is true. Still, I felt it was important and kept pressing. All the while, I was in excruciating pain. I couldn't move at all—not my legs, not my back, nothing.

I began to cough. The nurses warned me that coughing might burst my stitches, but I couldn't help it. The coughs became racking, full-body ordeals. Every time I coughed, sharp pains shot through my wound.

I couldn't breathe. I was coughing because I just couldn't get enough air. I grabbed a towel, rolled it up and put it over my incision. Sure enough, I was hacking so hard that my stitches burst. I went into my first surgery after the C-section to get re-stitched.

After that, I thought, **Well, now we're all set.** Little did I realize that this would be the first of many surgeries. I wasn't coughing for nothing; I was coughing because I had a clot in one of my arteries. The doctors would also discover a hematoma, a collection of blood outside of the blood vessels, in my abdomen, then even more clots that had to be kept from traveling to my lungs. That's what the medical report says, anyways. To me, it was just a fog of surgeries, one after another.

My husband left—to get food and a shower back at the house—and this started a trend in which every time he'd try to leave, I'd wind up back in the operating room. I had to get a second surgery, and before he could get home, he had to come right back. When I woke up from that surgery, in the hospital room with my parents and my in-laws, I felt like I was dying. They were trying to talk to me and all I could think was **I'm dying, I'm dying. Oh my god.** I really thought I would faint. I got up somehow and I went into the other room because I didn't want my mom to worry. I didn't want her to hear me; she's the world's biggest worrier.

In the other room, I spoke to the nurse. I told her: "I need to have a CAT scan of my lungs bilaterally, and then I need to be on my heparin drip." She said, "I think all this medicine is making you talk crazy." I said, "No, I'm telling you what I need, I need the scan immediately. And I need it to be done with dye." I guess I said the name of the dye wrong, and she told me I just needed to rest. But I persisted: "I'm telling you, this is what I need." I fought hard and I ended up getting the CAT scan. Finally the nurse called my doctor and she listened to me and insisted we check. I'm so grateful to her. Lo and behold, I had a blood clot in one lung, and they needed to insert a filter into my veins to break up the clot before it reached my heart.

Surgery number three. Something I never knew: Athletes have bigger veins. I was under for a long time because they could not find a filter to fit in my veins. The filter that fits every other patient wouldn't fit me.

Poor Alexis. He tried again to leave for a moment

at home, but they found another blood clot. He was distraught—and the man needed a shower! But back to the hospital he went, and I went in for surgery number four. I went into the same operating room so many times that I started to say, "I'm baaaaaack!" each time they wheeled me in. Alexis—and I can barely say this without laughing myself into tears—gave up on trying to leave. He showered in the hospital room because he was terrified to walk out the door. He didn't try again, and I didn't have any more surgeries.

Needless to say, I was exhausted. Despite fighting for it, I didn't like being on the heparin drip. I just wanted to be with my baby. I remained calm through it all, but afterwards, when everyone was retelling the story, I thought, **Wow, no wonder everyone was panicking.** My mother, my sister, my good friend Jill Smoller, my father—they were having their own mini heart attacks at my side. And I was just sitting there, telling the nurse what I needed. I had a totally different experience from everyone else. I was hiding my fear so well in the room that I didn't even feel it, while other people were hiding their fear from me in another room. It's a good thing I didn't realize that I was doing so poorly—panicking would've made everything worse.

My personal ob-gyn was amazing. She never made me feel dismissed. Another doctor was supposed to be checking in but I didn't see him very much. In fact, I saw him only once.

In the U.S., Black women are nearly three times more likely to die during or after childbirth than their white counterparts. Many of these deaths are considered by experts to be preventable. Being heard and appropriately treated was the difference between life or death for me; I know those statistics would be different if the medical establishment listened to every Black woman's experience.

A week later, I finally left the hospital with Olympia. In the span of seven days, I had gone through five surgeries back-to-back, including my C-section. My ob-gyn came every day for a month to stuff my C-section wound. She had to come and clean it because by then, I'd had so many surgeries that I wasn't able to do it myself. One side of the incision was so bad it wouldn't close. I returned to the hospital in November for another procedure to take out the filter. For whatever reason, that operation knocked me out worse than the others. For two weeks, I couldn't get my life together.

My body, my entire being was just so tired at that point. When I first got home, I couldn't walk down the driveway. When I finally made it to a tree half-way down the driveway, it was a big hurdle for me. Everyone in my family cheered me on, telling me, "You're doing so good!" They must've been aching on the inside, but they still all acted like nothing was wrong. My dad was so encouraging, saying, "Look, you did it!" This, after he coached me for years, all tough and relentless. I'm glad they didn't let me see how bad it really was.

Despite my body's wreckage—and the fact that I couldn't get in much breastfeeding—connecting with Olympia at long last was amazing; it was both the reward and the validation for all I'd been through. I went from not being able to really imagine her in the womb to us being completely inseparable. I still feel like I have to be around her for every day of her life, as much as possible. I'm anxious when I'm not around her. Honestly, it's a little much!

Olympia has a great sense of humor. If you tell her to draw a bunny, she'll draw a chicken instead, and she knows she's making a joke. She loves to laugh. I thought I was going to be really strict, but so far I'm the more lenient parent. This kid has me under her finger. I didn't know what kind of mom I'd be, and I still don't know. Instead, maybe for the first time in my life, I'm just **being**.

I Ran for the Delivery Guy's Wife

ALYSIA MONTAÑO

Olympic Runner

You might know me as the "Pregnant Runner" or the "Flying Flower." In 2014, while thirty-four weeks pregnant with my first child, Linnea, I ran the 800 meters at the USATF Outdoor Championships, finishing about thirty-five seconds slower than my personal best from four years prior in Monaco. I'd been competing in this particular race since 2006, and I wasn't about to miss it just because I was weeks away from giving birth.

I ran pregnant, with the approval of my doctor and midwife, for many reasons. To begin with, it was simply my reality: I was a mother, but I was still an athlete. I wanted to show the world—and myself—what it was like to pursue career goals and be a mother at the same time. I wanted people to see me running, with a yellow flower in my hair and a big tummy that realigned my center of gravity, and be inspired to not deny any part of their identities. I am a runner who happened to be pregnant; maybe you're a lawyer who happens to be pregnant, or an astronaut, or a cashier.

Another reason I ran? For the delivery guy's wife. While I was pregnant and prepping for the baby's arrival, I had a nonstop flow of stuff coming from Amazon, among other retailers, so the delivery guy and I got to know each other fairly well. He'd see me lacing up to go out for a run, and he'd say, "Are you **sure** you should do that?" It wasn't anything I hadn't heard before. Early on in my pregnancy, I posted a workout on Instagram and someone commented, "You're going to kill your kid." I was shocked. I didn't want anyone telling me how to take care of myself or my baby. I'd gotten the thumbs-up from my midwife to run throughout my entire pregnancy, because it's what my body was used to doing. Exercising is good for mother and baby. I stopped posting workouts after that, but the harsh comment stayed in my mind.

One day, I got new shoes and a uniform delivered. The uniform was for the Nationals, but I was still hesitating to register. My sponsor had already said to me, "You're not racing this year, right?" and I was like "Actually, I need a new uniform. Make it a medium or maybe a large." So the delivery guy was passing that package to me when he said, "You know, when my wife was pregnant, she was working out, but I made her stop."

I paused, about to just dismiss him with an **OK, cool,** but instead I said, "You know what? Probably what she needed from you more than anything else was your encouragement." Then I set off on my run, leaving him in the dust to think about that. Any hesitation I had about registering for the race was gone. I was going to run for **all** the women who had been told they couldn't exercise while pregnant. I wasn't running with an "injury," which is the way the running world sees pregnancy, by the way. I was running at my most beautiful and strong.

When I crossed the finish line on race day, I received a standing ovation. Running is my therapy, so I was already on a high but that reaction, well, it was incredible. Then the footage of me running went viral across the globe. My fans, the whole track-and-field world, and everyone else saw not only me but all of us mothers, everywhere, doing all the powerful things we do every day at our jobs.

The sponsors, who make it financially possible for athletes like me to train and participate in races, tell little girls they can be and do anything they want. Too bad that's not the message you'll get as an adult female athlete. When athletes get pregnant their contracts are often halted. Boom, no more pay, just like that. The National Olympic Committee paused my health insurance. My colleagues, Allyson Felix and Kara Goucher, experienced similar treatment from Nike but I had no idea at the time. I only thought, **Wow, look at the comeback those women made after pregnancy.** I didn't know about the discrimination or the total lack of support that they dealt with—so often we women suffer in silence.

Having a baby and training for the Olympics are not that different, at least for me. As my due date with Linnea loomed, I trained with positions I thought would benefit me in childbirth, like squats. I'd hold the squat for the longest interval I could manage. I was lucky that my pregnancy was without any serious problems. I did have Pubic Symphysis Dysfunction, which happens in some 60 percent of pregnancies, but the pain went away by twenty weeks or so.

At first, my husband, Louis, wanted a home birth. I told him that with the first kid, I just wasn't ready for the home birth experience, though I do think it sounds lovely. He and I have always been able to discuss anything. We've known each other since high school, so there's a real level of comfort between us. I was never the girl who dreamed about her wedding day, but I did dream of having a big family. I have one brother but so many cousins whom I'm close to that I often say I have six brothers. Growing up, I had lots of aunts and uncles around too, because my mother was one of ten. It was very much the it-takes-a-village setup in our family; everyone had a hand in raising us.

Anyway, when I dreamed of a big family, my

vision was to have up to four kids. Louis and I discussed the timeline of it all. My body is my business, so planning was crucial. Having babies would have to align with my career. The best plan would be giving birth in an off year, when I wouldn't be running at Nationals to qualify for an Olympic or world championship team. Luckily, I got pregnant quickly and we were able to make that happen.

After the home birth idea was set aside, I set my sights on an unmedicated hospital birth with as few interventions as possible. Let me say that I don't think unmedicated is the best or only way to have a baby, and I would never call it "natural birth." All birth is natural! But a big selling point for this kind of birth, for me, was that I could use it as a unique training experience. Accomplishing an unmedicated birth would actually strengthen and condition me, mentally and physically, for the next race in a way that lifting weights or running sprints could never do. Birth, I figured, would be the greatest athletic performance I'd ever be part of—and if I could get through it on my own, I knew I could get through anything. I made sure I had a midwife at my side, just like I would work with a coach for the Olympics. I took every precaution to make sure I'd be safe: It wasn't lost on me that Black women die at a much higher rate than white women in childbirth. Biases exist within the medical world, I'm well aware, and I was not about to become a statistic.

I was just hitting forty weeks when my water

broke—I mean **exploded**—in the shower. Was it all the chili I ate? The five miles I ran earlier in the day? I didn't know, but I couldn't believe that much water came out of me. I laughed hysterically. My husband then rushed in and we both couldn't stop laughing. The midwife told me over the phone to drink some orange juice and wait for the show to begin.

After eating more chili, watching **Curb Your Enthusiasm**, and listening to some meditation music, the contractions got intense at about 7:30 in the evening (my water had broken at 2:30). Around 10:30 P.M., my mom showed up at our door, having taken a flight from L.A. (where I grew up, in Santa Clarita) to the Bay Area. I told her to go for a drive; I was too in the zone to talk to her. She drove to pick up my aunt Maxine and then went to CVS for snacks. Then I told her she had to come back right away: It was time to go to the hospital.

She sped back to us and, of course, got pulled over. A person of color always has to be so careful not to set off the cop, so my mom patiently explained the situation but the cop didn't believe her. She said, "Can I show you my phone?" He wasn't having it. She begged, "Please, let me show you my phone." Finally, he let her and there was my text: "WHERE ARE YOU?!"

For her, that text couldn't have come at a better time. The cop was like, "Go!" No ticket. She pulled up outside the house, where I was waiting on the sidewalk in my robe, holding my birth ball. We didn't get to the hospital until 12:30.

By 1:20 A.M., holding on to the wall in the shower, I told my husband, "Okay, I see why people get epidurals." At this point, I was seeing stars but trying to keep loose and fluid. He was like, "You can do this." I had told him previously to not let me get an epidural unless I used a safe word or something. I told him, "You'll just know if I really need one." The nurse popped her head in and said, "Did you say you want an epidural?" I was like, "No! Don't say that word!" I knew I was close to having this baby and I just had to drag myself over that finish line. No one else thought I was close; my midwife wasn't even there yet.

The nurse checked my cervix and said, "We need a doctor." Then she nervously asked, "How do you want to give birth?" And I was like, "I don't know. How do people do it?" Luckily, my midwife ran in just as the baby was crowning. A few minutes later, Linnea was born, about twelve hours after my water broke.

I was in love right away. I was just in absolute awe of her, how beautiful she was. I asked the nurse, "Is this baby beautiful or am I just that parent?" And she dutifully answered, "Your baby is beautiful." I'd never seen anything so precious and amazing. Everything in me just melted.

At home, my whole family had come into town

but I just wanted to be with Linnea. We were in such newborn bliss. She was a great breastfeeder, but I had lots of problems with engorgement. I'm a super-producer and my boobs basically filled up with milk to my neck and out to my armpits. At about three weeks postpartum, right when her sleep started to really go awry (she would wake up about once an hour . . . in other words, torture), I started to have what my mom called the "baby blues." I just felt so sad all the time. Those feelings prompted me to move back closer to my family in Santa Clarita. I needed their help, especially if I wanted to run again. Thankfully, the depressive feelings passed quickly.

The biggest challenge of all was reentering the work world. When I was a few months postpartum, I had a call with my sponsor at the time. I had a good rapport with the prior athletic manager (a woman), but on my first phone call with these two new guys, they informed me that they'd need to reduce my contract by 50 percent due to my "performance" last year. "You mean the year I was pregnant?" I asked. Yep, they sure did.

Despite all my former accomplishments—a six-time USA Outdoor champion, an Olympian, a record holder for the 600 meters in America—they doubted me. They didn't think I could return to form after my pregnancy. I proved them wrong. I won a national championship at six months postpartum. I won another national championship at ten months postpartum while still nursing my baby girl. I showed up to the World Championships in Beijing, China, still nursing, and pumped for ten days, shipping my milk back to my daughter in the States. For months, my schedule was one big cycle of pumping, nursing, running, napping, eating, and weight training. None of this would've been possible without Louis, who had agreed to be the primary parent at home. For my sponsor, though, none of this was good enough. They cut my contract not long after I tripped and fell at the 2016 Olympic Trials, forgoing my chance of getting on the team. It felt like they had been just **waiting** for me to make a mistake.

In 2017, when I was five months pregnant with my son Aster, I ran again in the national championships because it's not like much had changed since 2014. Not having any system in place to protect female athletes puts our health at risk. In 2019, on Mother's Day, I spoke out against Nike's policies (and ASICS', and so many others) in a **New York Times** op-ed. The response was astounding: Less than two weeks after the article ran, Nike announced that it would waive pay reductions based on performance for a year after an athlete gives birth. The company added that in 2018, "we standardized our approach" so that women wouldn't be penalized. A few months after that op-ed, I got offers from companies that actually valued **all** sides of me: the mother and the athlete. I eventually signed with Cadenshae, a maternity activewear company, and now I have my own clothing line in development with them, called Bloom. Together we want to change the standard for athletic apparel. We value mothers and their ability to bloom and evolve—that's a mother's superpower, not her hindrance. We want athletics to be an inclusive space for mothers, where they can be supported and protected. Hopefully, more companies will follow suit.

Fortunately, there are other brands that have stepped up to support me. Altra Running signed me when I was pregnant with my third. I believe their sponsorship will extend beyond me, as one athlete who can now continue her career. Alta Running is cutting a path for other brands to follow. When one of us gets a chance to excel as her full, magnificent self, then it's possible for all of us.

So, things are changing, but there's always more work to be done. There needs to be **legislative** change. I want to see federally mandated maternity protections for women, both in and out of sports, and so I've started a nonprofit, &Mother, to further that cause. My upward climb has made one thing abundantly clear: I won't allow a brand or even a piece of gold to dictate what I do with my family, when or **if** I should have more kids. In February 2020, I gave birth to my third child, my son Lennox. He's perfect, but that doesn't mean I'm about to have a fourth. **Hell no.** I'm so grateful for the three of them. It's the perfect team for us.

The Advocate
ABBY G. LOPEZ
Doula

I've worked as a doula in the New York area since 2018, assisting many women before, during, and after labor. Every time I've helped my clients give birth, what the women experience is transformative for them. Becoming a mother is an incredible moment—though it's one that I know purely as a birth worker and not as a mother. (I prefer to be a doting aunt to many nieces and nephews.) For me, the most transformative birth I've ever experienced was my very first experience as a doula, and it's seared into my memory. I was helping Blanca,* a woman from Nicaragua, give birth to her third child at a hospital in New York City. Her birth plan was to be

---

*Not her real name.

up and walking around for as long as possible, but her labor had progressed quickly and when I arrived, her water had already broken and she'd passed meconium. The hospital-assigned midwife and nurse instructed her that she had to stay on the bed with a fetal monitor. She was also hooked up to an IV. Once bedridden, Blanca no longer had the advantage of gravity to assist her in labor. I'm convinced this played a part in how things unfolded.

I could tell from the moment I walked in that Blanca and her husband were not comfortable. Everything about this labor was different from her first two unmedicated births in Nicaragua. That culture shock was a lot to experience while giving birth. They did not speak English, and I knew that the hospital staff hadn't fully explained all the big mysterious machines hooked up to her. It was all foreign to them. I knew that stress wasn't good for Blanca or the baby, and I wanted to help them.

I've worked in health and wellness for twenty years. I became a doula as a natural extension of my work as a massage therapist and yoga instructor. My prenatal massage clients often requested that I help them with their labor. In 2018, I completed my training with Ancient Song Doula Services, which focuses on offering doula services to all families, regardless of their socioeconomic standing. They are also committed to addressing implicit bias and racism within healthcare. Through Ancient Song, I learned aspects of women's history that I'd never studied in school.

I learned about the forced sterilization of Puerto Rican women from the 1930s to the '70s. The United States used sterilization as a weapon of population control: A 1965 survey of Puerto Rican residents found that about one-third of all Puerto Rican mothers, ages twenty to forty-nine, were sterilized. I'm a Latina—my parents are from Puerto Rico and I grew up in East New York, Brooklyn—so this was my **own** history and even I didn't know any of this.

U.S. history is rife with stories of forced sterilizations of non-white women in particular. Throughout the twentieth century, more than sixty thousand people were sterilized under U.S. eugenics programs, which were federally funded in thirty-two states. Between 1930 and 1970, 85 percent of the 7,600-plus sterilizations ordered by the state of North Carolina were carried out on Black women. As many as 25 percent of Native American women between fifteen and forty-four years old were sterilized during the 1970s.

Sterilization is still used today—in 2020, nurse Dawn Wooten accused ICE of allegedly forcing hysterectomies on women at a Georgia detention center. But there was another statistic on my mind on the day that I was helping Blanca: The U.S. has the world's highest maternal mortality rate for a developed nation. It's the worst for non-white women; Asians, Latinas, and Black women are all more likely to die than their white counterparts.

With all that on my mind, I was worried for Blanca, but I had hope that everything would be okay.

She was thirty, healthy, and had given birth before. These were all positive signs. After a few hours of labor, she asked for an epidural. I translated Blanca's request for the nurse and was shocked when she sniped, "Well, I guess that whole birth plan is going out the window." The judgmental response took me aback, but I let it go. I didn't want to stress Blanca further by escalating tension with the nurse. The anesthesiologist came in to perform the epidural, but with barely a glance at Blanca and me, he demanded a translator. I'd been paired with Blanca through Ancient Song, to act, in part, as a translator. I speak Spanish very well and had worked for NYU for several years as a clinical technician and translated there all the time. But the anesthesiologist didn't care. He just saw two brown women and walked out of the room.

A Spanish-speaking nurse came in and, tensely, we navigated the conversation. Not long after Blanca got the epidural (the anesthesiologist wouldn't let me stay in the room), she was almost fully dilated; the resident left to get the OB. For a long time, Blanca only had me and a nurse helping her into stirrups and telling her to push. The doctors were nowhere to be seen.

Finally, the resident returned and checked Blanca again. I saw her purse her lips with a look of impatience and then she snapped at Blanca in a way I found very unprofessional. "Well, nothing has happened. You haven't dilated any further. What's going on? Are you not pushing?" she demanded.

I stopped translating because I didn't like the resident's tone. Instead I pushed back against the resident, saying, "Look, she's pushing, she's working really hard. She's in a lot of pain." As I was speaking, the attending doctor came into the room. Interrupting me, the resident told him: "She hasn't dilated any further. I don't know what's going on. It's just poor maternal effort."

"Poor maternal effort"? I was stunned. I'd never heard of this term. It sounded so awful, and it wasn't accurate to the situation. My heart broke for Blanca. When I looked at her, I saw her courage, her dedication to being a good mother, and I saw how much she loved her baby already. She was dealing with culture shock, a language barrier, physical pain, and these doctors were treating her like it was her fault the baby wasn't out yet. Nobody cared about her as a person; she was just a body that they wanted to get out of their way. Because Blanca was Latinx and an immigrant—a legal immigrant, for the record, not that it should matter—she was being treated in that hospital like a second-class citizen. I knew what discrimination looked like, but I had not expected to find it here.

I knew I had to step in, to help protect Blanca. I told the resident that the numbing of the epidural might be making it difficult for Blanca to feel where to push. The resident, with her fingers in Blanca's vagina, pushed down and snapped, "Tell her to push here, right here." The resident started barking directly at Blanca, even knowing that Blanca wouldn't understand. I saw the fear in Blanca's face and told the resident to please try and relax her tone a little bit.

The OB stepped in then, and without asking, stuck his fingers in Blanca. He tried to move the baby around, but nothing happened. Blanca was exhausted. She said to me, "I think I need a C-section." It was my job to keep her comfortable, to support her, and I assured her that we'd work this out. I had faith she could do it but at the same time, this was my very first experience as a doula and I wasn't sure how we'd get this baby out without surgery.

By the grace of God, the midwife walked in. She had been there when I'd first arrived, but had quickly been called away on another birth. I updated her, and she briskly took command of the situation. "No, we don't need a C-section. Give me ten minutes." The OB stepped back and the midwife and I turned Blanca onto her left side. I held up her right leg and as soon as she turned, the baby's head came out. My breath caught. I'd never seen this part of a birth before. And I was relieved for Blanca. Finally, the baby was coming!

Blanca started to push and the midwife said, "Let's turn the other way." So we helped her onto her right side and just like that, the baby came all the way out. It turned out to be so simple. I felt a flood of relief; I can only imagine what Blanca felt. As soon as someone had listened to Blanca and treated her with care, all we had to do was move her around a little bit and the baby slipped right out. The baby's head, because the doctor had been grabbing it and trying to pull him down, was elongated, almost like forceps had been used. The OB examined the baby and said he must've been stuck behind her pubic bone. I couldn't help getting a little salty and commented that it wasn't "poor maternal effort" after all. The doctor seemed uncomfortable. I could tell that kind of comment wouldn't get made again.

Nevertheless, the resident came back in. Instead of allowing the placenta to come out naturally, she started pulling it out. If the placenta tears internally, it can be toxic for the mom. It can kill her. So, to me, it just seemed like, again, they wanted Blanca out of there as soon as possible. I watched carefully to make sure all of the placenta came out intact.

Blanca was okay in the end; she got to meet her healthy baby boy and avoided a C-section. Before I left, I found the midwife and thanked her. I said, "I feel like she was getting beat up in there and if it wasn't for you, I don't know what would've happened." The midwife answered, "Oh, one hundred percent she was getting beat up in there. And that's why you and I need to do what we do."

In the room, my job had been to stay strong and take care of Blanca. But once I got back to my car, I lost it. I gripped the steering wheel and sobbed for a long time. Blanca had been treated so badly by the doctors, and the fact that everything had ended up okay didn't make what had happened along the way acceptable. When I could see through my tears to drive, I went home to my longtime partner. When I got home, he was waiting for me. I'd left in the middle of the night and hadn't picked up my phone for hours. He asked, "How did it go?" And I just burst into tears again. I told him everything and after seeing the shock on his face, I realized what the role of a doula truly is. It's not only to comfort and guide the mother, it's to be her advocate. To make sure that her voice is being heard. That day with Blanca made me realize that I needed to do this work so that, at the very least, I could prevent a patient from being treated like trash again. What would've happened to Blanca if I hadn't been there? Would she have had any voice at all?

In the years that followed my first experience as a doula, I've helped many women with their deliveries. It is demanding work, spiritually and physically. It was Blanca's birth that transformed me, and made me understand my calling and my purpose. I'll never forget Blanca, her baby boy, and how they were treated by the healthcare system. And I'll never let that happen to another mother again.

The Disembarkment
AMBER TAMBLYN
Author and Actress

There it was. In broad daylight, on a Sunday, in the bathroom, resting on top of my husband's face towel, which was probably not really something he used for his face. I stared down at it, a mixture of electrified thrill and complete terror surging through my entire body. My pants were still down around my ankles and a glass of warm piss sat on the counter next to me, something I would later mistake for a glass of water in the middle of the night and take a sip from. If you're curious what room temp urine tastes like, it's quite shocking and surreal, like the feeling you get the exact moment you learn you're pregnant. There it was, staring back up at me with its two beady pink lines: a pregnancy test that was positive.

For the longest time, my thoughts around conceiving—both making a baby and wrapping my head around making one—were tethered to the instability I experienced growing up as a child actress in the entertainment business, a career which started at the age of ten. And though I've had a writing career equally as tenured, having written many books over the years, my career as an actress was what was most important about me to other people. As an adult, there was always a constant, nagging fear that the lack of normalcy in my childhood would manifest as some unchecked resentment toward any child of mine who would likely have the freedoms I did not. Plus, it's no secret that Hollywood has a rich history of punishing women who don't stay the traditional desirability course: women who are outspoken, women who dare to age gracefully, women of color, in general, and women who have sworn off the identity of ingénues to become (gasp!) mothers. There was Dana Plato, star of the beloved '70s sitcom **Diff'rent Strokes,** who was fired from the show after getting pregnant out of wedlock, an event so traumatic some would say it led to her death at the devastatingly young age of thirty-four. There are the stories of abused and drugged young Judy Garlands, and the stories of Michelle Pfeiffers taking time off to raise kids only to return to an industry that had replaced them with younger, less motherly Michelle Pfeiffers. These types of truths about my profession created heavy psychic weight behind every personal decision I made, or tried to avoid making altogether. The road to accepting and wanting a future of motherhood was, without question, fraught.

Years earlier in 2008, I had fallen madly in love with my then boyfriend, David Cross (now husband), and we moved in together after dating for just five months. There was definitely lag time between nights of unprotected sex after East Village bar crawls, and finally getting on birth control. The lag time wasn't one I had given much thought to—I was in my twenties and my life was in a holding pattern of irresponsible choices. I believed myself invisible to the realities of what consequences could, and did, come my way.

A few days after moving in with David, I left to go on tour with my writing partner and best friend of fifteen years, the poet Derrick Brown, and our mutual friend, the photographer Matt Wignall. We were headed for a show in Oklahoma, Derrick on his motorcycle and me and Matt in a U-Haul (it's a long story) when I began to feel ill. The drive was long with many stops in between, and at every new truck stop or Cracker Barrel, the pain in my lower abdomen worsened. By the time we reached the land of rolling hills and fried okra, it was clear that Derrick would be performing without me and that I might need to go to the hospital. We dropped Derrick off at the venue at sunset and I stumbled out of the passenger seat to lie facedown in a nearby patch of grass that had been baked all day by the sun. The warm earth felt so good on my stomach and I pressed my body into it as another rolling, brutal cramp broke over me. Derrick looked down at me, a box of books and merchandise in his hands, worried. "Don't die on me, buddy," he said, half joking. I gave him a thumbs-up and groaned into the hot dirt.

By the time Matt got me to the hotel and up to the room, I was pale and drenched in sweat. We both agreed that if I didn't turn a corner soon, I needed to go to an emergency room. When I got up from the bed to use the bathroom, a new sensation flooded over me, as if something other than pee wanted to come out of me—wanted to be released from my body immediately. I sat on the toilet and gripped the sides of the seat. **What is happening to me?** I thought. And then another voice chimed in. **Push.** So I pushed. I trembled and groaned. **Push, Amber. Push,** I told myself. Matt knocked on the door to see if I was okay. I wheezed out a yes, just as an electric current shot down my legs, followed by an audible **plop** in the water beneath me. I leaned back against the toilet seat and cried big, ugly, heaving sobs as the cramps began to dissipate. **My god,** I thought, **what the fuck was that?** Weak, I got up and peered at what looked like a small fist of blood floating in the water, surrounded by long strands of what I could only imagine were pieces of my body's tissue. I didn't know what it was, what to do with it—show it to Matt? Gross—so I flushed and crawled back into bed, thoroughly exhausted. I told Matt I was going to be okay, but he stayed there with me well into the night just to make sure.

I was perhaps too young, or too naive, to know then that what happened to me that day was likely a miscarriage. I didn't come to understand this until many years later when my doctor asked about prior medical history and I flippantly recalled a coo-coo-bananas time ten years ago when my vagina shit out a mini cupcake of blood in an Oklahoma Days Inn toilet. She said it could've been a miscarriage, but unless I had gotten tested at a hospital right after it had happened, there was just no way to know for sure.

But I know for sure. I know it was a miscarriage.

The day after my miscarriage, I got out of bed, achy and still tired, and proceeded to pack my bags as if it was just another hangover. No biggie! Back to bourbon and poetry nights on the road! I joked to friends about that strange day in Oklahoma, making light of it whenever I could. Like most women, we know it's better to just keep moving, past the truth and pain of our experience. But as I got older, the consequences of the disconnect between my body and unprocessed childhood trauma would not be so easy to bounce back from.

Years later, I found myself at the end of a very long existential rope, and in crisis about the trajectory of my life. David and I had just gotten married, yet I was more unsure about my career than ever. I was stuck, completely paralyzed between the identity of being an actress for hire, and the woman who longed to become more than just that—a woman who wanted to direct movies, write lots of books, and produce television shows. Could I be all of these things? And also a mother? The answer in my mind at that time was no.

Things got more difficult when David and I found out I was pregnant, and I made the decision to terminate the pregnancy. I made the appointment for January 2, telling myself it would be a New Year's resolution of some kind, something to drastically change this holding pattern of mine, this negligent, self-involved half-ass way of living.

When I woke up from the operation, the nurse gave me a Jell-O cup and some Advil. The doctor told me everything had gone well and I was released after the anesthesia wore off. I clutched the discharge papers to my chest and limped toward the elevator, feeling like a Molotov cocktail of relief and brokenness. Outside the building, an older man stood at a respectful distance from the entrance and handed me a pamphlet that loudly screamed, "CHOOSE LIFE!" I took the pamphlet from his hands and told him, "I just did."

For many years that followed the miscarriage in Oklahoma and the terminated pregnancy in New York City, I took that resolution seriously, dedicating much of my time to healing and growing. I started therapy and worked through many of the traumas of my past. I began to feel more like the authentic version of who I was always meant to become. I directed a film, published books, and still acted when there was an opportunity to play something I loved. I felt comfortable in my own skin, and I knew I was ready to become a mom.

After nine long months of indigestion, exhaustion, and daily, uncharacteristic cravings for Oreo cookies, I was ready to welcome our baby into the world. The day of my scheduled C-section delivery, I waddled into the hospital with David at an ungodly hour and checked myself in. A few hours later, after a bevy of IVs had been inserted in my hands and blood had been drawn, I was brought into the operating room by my two doctors, Lee and Karen. David wasn't allowed to come in for the initial part of the surgery—apparently partners often faint or get sick to their stomachs after watching the person they love opened up like a common ziplock bag full of stewed tomatoes—so I went in alone while he anxiously waited outside the door. Lee had me sit on an operating table where a very large bright light loomed overhead. My legs dangled over the edge and Karen told me to round my lower back by leaning forward, making room for the insertion of the epidural needle in my lower spine. I couldn't stop shaking, with equal parts fear and excitement. Karen came close and grabbed ahold of my hands tightly. She pointed at her forehead and directed me in her strong New York accent to put my forehead against hers, so I did. She whispered a reminder: Women have been doing this since the beginning of mankind. We are powerful— more powerful than we know.

The epidural had kicked in and I was lying flat on

my back with a sheet separating me from my lower body, which I could no longer feel. David came in and sat by my side. I asked him to make inappropriate jokes while the sound of suctioned blood and the smell of burning flesh wafted around us. All he could muster was a sad joke about a Merlot cart coming by to serve wine. That's how bad I knew it all was. In between requests by Lee for scalpels, and busy nurses running around with medical instruments, I flashed through a series of memories that had led up to this moment. **My abnormal childhood. Going to work after school while other kids got to play. Awful auditions with perverted directors. Starving myself for a week before an award show. Blood in the toilet in Oklahoma. Holding patterns. Drinking too much. Crying in therapy. Taking the East River ferry home alone after having my abortion. My husband's devastated face. More crying in therapy. My husband's joyous face, in this moment as I give birth. My life. My future, finally here.**

And then, there it was. In broad operating room light. On a Wednesday. Lifted up by my doctor over a blue curtain, right in front of my very eyes: my daughter, born. My daughter, so small and real and alive; a tender new heart pulsing outside of my body, free, fully her own.

"Oh," I cried out when I saw her.

"There you are. **There you are.**"

Marlow Alice Cross had finally arrived. And so had I.

The Song of the Three Bodies, Singing

A poem for my miscarriage, my abortion, and my daughter, Marlow

BY AMBER TAMBLYN

Author and Actress

1.
Imagine the body giving in to another one leaving it,
and a brain that didn't know it did. Imagine what haunts
a ghost, what premonition still lingers in the space
between knowing and believing. Imagine what keeps
   the body
separated from its shadow at night, what sound taught
   the wolves
never to obey.

Imagine what you didn't want but were given anyway.
It is a song only you were meant to hear. A pain for
   only you
to feel, far after the fact. It is a story you can never
   give back,
a living you will find a way to get through.

So forgive me, body, for not hearing. Forgive me, as a
    woman
they taught my bones never to listen
to my blood.

When I was younger, I was taught to bullseye the target
of my teens, to arrow down the softest parts of my
    hunter.
I was taught to carnage my instinct, stand out by never
    standing down.

And now all I can do, all I can dream about
is who the clouds were sent for. Who's haunting the ghosts
will walk through walls for. Why a shadow returns
with or without its sun. All I can think about
is what the Earth must've seen that day
that I could not.

Forgive me, body, for not seeing. Forgive me, as a woman
they taught my heart never to watch out
for my pulse.

Imagine with me now; the red glass that broke inside me
like a lightbulb's flood slipping to its final shatter, still lit.
Imagine the light you caused, the damage
you did to the dark that day you surrendered
from me.

Remember what a shard can do. Open you
to a window that can never be closed. Open you

to the dawning of what you can and can't control.
   Open you
to palms outstretched. Letting go.

2.
In the operating room, I stared up into a fluorescent hell
and said the only prayer I'd ever believe is true.
When I'm ready to love you, come back to me.
When I'm ready to know you, come back to my body.

My eyes closed to blackness and I met you there,
in the nothing between us, a flame curtailed
between our suffering. I met you there in the quiet
   dark
of all the bad spells I have bound to myself.

I met you there, outside of my body but still within.
I met you there, alone and afraid, but never unsure.
You were the ricochet of my youthful unruliness,
the reins my rough edges could not reel in.

When I'm ready to love you, come back to me.
When I'm ready to know you, come back to my body.

My eyes closed and I pictured you: Small as a saffron seed
growing auburn inside of me. I saw you as a gift
I would someday open with different hands.
I saw you strong, loud, living in a world full of love
given by a mother who could offer it
unconditionally.

When it was done, and my eyes cracked open
to a room full of kerosene women dowsed in their guilt's
    flames,
I could feel your absence, but never your abandonment.
I could feel your absence, but never your abandonment.
I could feel your absence, but never your abandonment.

Because I met you there, in the something between us
in the only prayer I'd ever believe is true.

You'll come back to me, as I to you.
You'll know me, and my body
will one day know you.

3.
You arrived as a rebirth's overture.
The sonic boom of my heart's aching flutter.
You arrived as the reason behind, the reason for, the
    reason of,
the only reason.

You arrived as a tilt toward hysterical bliss,
an ellipsis from crack in my hips,
a dawn awoken from the ancients
stationed in my ribs.

You arrived, the answer.
The cure. The fear. The dread.
The sorrow. The shock. The joy.

The joy. The joy. The joy. **The joy.**

You arrived,
my surrender's proclamation.
My crowned tidal.
You arrived,
my radiant, wild, fearless child,
holy-charged, the only church
for which I bow to an altar.

You arrived and I knew
beyond the blackouts in Texas bars,
and lost car keys in Kentucky trash cans,

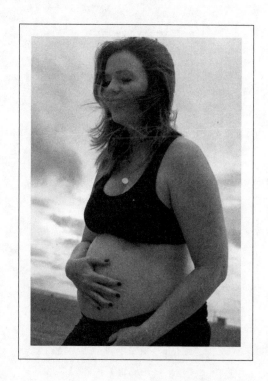

and fistfights and breakups,
beyond the one
who was never worthy of us
and the other one
who was never ready for us,
beyond the letdowns and give-ups,
the give-ins and dropouts,

you arrived and I know. I know
you were always here.
You were always
home.

A Third Chance

SHILPA SHAH

Entrepreneur

The hospital where I was delivering was a ghost town. Outside, a few days after George Floyd's death, the streets were roiling. Black Lives Matter protestors were marching in cities around the country, including Oakland and Berkeley, where we live. By contrast, the hospital was eerily quiet. The staff, all in masks, were tensely waiting for a tsunami of COVID-19 patients.

For the birth of our third child, I was trying for a VBAC, a vaginal birth after delivering my second son by an emergency C-section. I was incredibly lucky that I was able to have my husband with me in the delivery room; a month earlier, in April 2020, many women had to give birth without their partners present due to COVID protocols. I also got to forgo wearing a mask, thanks to a rapid-result negative test, but I was still nervous about the birth in general. Was the third going to come really fast, too fast for an epidural? Would the birth end in a C-section again? At home, my eleven-year-old and eight-year-old sons were terrified for me. Their mother was delivering a baby in the hospital with a deadly pandemic on the loose. The year before, for the first time, loss had crept into their lives: Their aunt, my husband's sister, passed away after a decades-long battle with alcoholism. Death was now a tangible reality to them.

Thankfully, my OB arranged for me to receive an epidural right away even though my contractions were far apart. Then we started Pitocin, which made the contractions come faster and pushed me to dilate. I was relieved to make progress. My friend, Dr. P., who was also an ob-gyn at the hospital, arrived to keep me company. She had performed the emergency C-section for my second child, an outcome that neither of us wanted, though he was healthy. As much as she could, she wanted to make sure this birth didn't go the same way.

The sense of community in the delivery room was beautiful, and all the more precious to me after months of social distancing. I had these two wonderful OBs, a staff of attentive nurses, and an anesthesiologist whose children went to school with ours. The love and support were palpable—I felt lifted by them. My husband would tell me later, when the nurses and the two OBs surrounded my bed, coaching me as I pushed, that he was in awe of this primal show of female strength and wisdom. It was the most beautiful, euphoric birth I'd ever experienced. To be honest, I'm not sure my husband needed to be there after all!

When my baby boy came out, he wriggled on my chest and latched right away. After they took him away to be bathed, I was supposed to nap, but I couldn't. Instead, this amazing sense of gratitude for my good fortune flooded my body; I sat awake in its thrall for hours. I'd been given another chance—in so many ways.

We named our third son Aarav, which means "peaceful composure." His brothers also have "A" names; my first, Amani, means "fulfillment" and his younger brother is Alekh, which means "that which cannot be written." Together, I hope these brown boys will be part of a changing world, one that restores peace and gives justice to all those denied it, the ones the protestors were fighting for a few miles away.

I almost didn't have Aarav. In fact, early on in my pregnancy, I went to see my OB—the same one who would end up delivering him—and told her I was considering an abortion. Before I became pregnant with him, after years of struggle, I'd finally reached a life equilibrium. As a co-founder of a fashion start-up, Cuyana, I'd spent the last seven years working long hours, missing my kids. My husband would plead, "You need to stop working so much," and I would assure him, "It'll ease up soon," but it never did. Finally, after my sister-in-law's death, I took a leave of absence. My husband was in tears every night; he couldn't function. My family needed me. And for the first time in years, I was fully available to Alekh and Amani, in the way that they needed. Now, at last, I was the kind of mother I hoped to be—and I was scared a third child would take away all of that.

That day in the OB's office, after I asked her what she thought I should do, have an abortion or carry this baby to term, she carefully said, "I don't know, but I can tell you're not ready to make this decision today." Over the next few weeks, it became clear that we wanted this baby. I'm pro-choice, but in this case, I didn't feel like we had a choice. We had a loving home and financial security—I only had to forgive myself for not always being the mother I'd wanted to be for Alekh and Amani. I only had to trust myself that I could be a good mother to them all.

When I was younger, being a good mother sounded like a trap. I didn't want to be one of those traditional Indian girls that made my life all about kids and marriage while my other dreams died. I wanted to accomplish more. Growing up, I was stringent about equality between the genders. If my mother wanted to teach me how to make roti, then Sandeep, my older brother, had to learn too. My father had left a community of Indians in Uganda when he was eighteen for school in London, so he was more familiar with Western ideals. I could appeal to his sense of fairness. My mother, on the other hand, wanted to teach me how to be a traditional Indian wife and mother because that's what happiness and real adulthood meant to her. She became my father's wife in an arranged marriage two weeks after meeting him. Then they moved to West Covina, outside of Los Angeles, where they knew no one. My parents would get out the phone book and call Indian names all over Southern California, with the hope of making friends. They stitched together a giant Indian community that way, and there were many families we saw for every holiday, every big life event.

In Hinduism, there are four stages of life, known as the "four **ashramas.**" I'm not very religious, but it's still a useful way of thinking about the world. After the first phase, the student phase, there's the **Grihastha** stage, where you are establishing yourself in the world, making money. I could always picture setting up my career when I was growing up, but the bulk of **Grihastha** is about leading a household. It literally means "being in and occupied with home and family" and that aspect of it I could never picture. I remember talking to my aunt, telling her that for the final **Sannyasa** stage, I'd be happy to leave everything behind for spiritual enlightenment. She gasped and said, "You would leave even if you had a family? You can't do that."

Then I met my husband at a hip-hop concert when I was twenty-two, and after some false starts, we started dating. Within a month, I knew he was the one. After the saga of my last relationship, five tumultuous years with a Muslim man who couldn't tell his family about me because they wouldn't approve, it struck me how easy it was with Swapnil from the start. That's my advice for anyone looking for partnership: It shouldn't be hard and dramatic in the early days. Marriage and having a family will throw so many challenges at you that it has to be easy in the beginning, because it's immensely difficult to survive the hardships later.

In the end, I followed my mother's dream to a T—I married an Indian doctor. The irony is hilarious. My rebelliousness served me only up to a point. And ultimately, people are not always what you expect them to be. My own mother, who was so scared I would deviate from the traditional path, ended up doing that herself in a certain way. The whole time she was raising me and Sandeep, she was an entrepreneur. Eventually, she became a loan officer and my family became very well-off because of her income.

The entrepreneur in her is definitely in me too. I studied interface design as an undergrad but when I wanted to understand more about the money side—why certain projects were successful and others weren't—I went back for my MBA. I was pregnant with my second and had a two-year-old at home during my second year at UC Berkeley's Haas School of Business. For the sake of networking with my peers, I learned how to dip into a party and nurse one weak drink in the time the others would have three. I didn't want to be regarded as Old Mom, so I participated early and often. I even let them draw on my big pregnant belly for fun; I just rolled with it all.

After graduation, I co-launched Cuyana, focusing on sustainable essentials, with a fellow fashion industry outsider, mathematician Karla Gallardo. We had to penetrate this market that we knew less about, which is part of the reason I worked so hard. I would go up to anyone at a conference, tap them on the shoulder and introduce myself. But the older my kids got, the harder it became to lose myself in the work. I became like a broken record, saying to Karla that I didn't need more money, I needed time. I needed more time at home. For years, Karla didn't quite get it—no one really understands the demands of family unless they have one themselves—but she started to empathize in a different way after having her first child.

My sister-in-law's passing was a tipping point. We got a call from the coroner's office about her death right after we'd bought a new house. We were still in the old one, half living out of boxes. With my husband in mourning, it was up to me to move us into the new house, fix up the old one, and tend to my kids. With Karla's blessing, I walked away for a few months.

For the first time in years, I was just there for them. The four of us were so connected, like we've never really been before. We took a road trip together, just me and the boys. Then all of us went to the Galápagos. For three months, life was slow. We were sifting through grief, but still, I was relaxed. Like, play-with-my-kids-for-hours-outside kind of relaxed. It's no surprise, looking back, that I got pregnant, but I was still stunned.

There is a sense of reincarnation in Hinduism, the idea that a soul returns to the physical realm in a new body. What percentage of women get accidentally pregnant at forty-one? While I don't believe this baby literally was my sister-in-law's spirit, I'll never know if getting pregnant with Aarav wasn't somehow the universe's way of moving us forward. The birth itself felt like a culmination of everything that came before: With my first, I had this amazing delivery, but I struggled to bond with the baby. For my second, I was super bonded to him but the

delivery had been traumatizing. For Aarav, it all came together—a beautiful delivery and an instant connection, in this tumultuous time in our country when so much else fell away, except the bonds of family and the importance of protecting each other.

Having Aarav pushed me to realize that I was capable of more than I thought. I got the chance to have another baby, but with all this newfound understanding of our family's pain, and our happiness, and how both could be encapsulated in one wonderful being. The larger picture finally came into focus.

A Calling

CHRISTY TURLINGTON BURNS

Maternal Health Advocate

Less than an hour after delivering my first child, Grace, a healthy baby girl, a complication arose: My placenta wasn't coming out. The nurses at the birth center had tried everything that was supposed to help it detach: massaging my abdomen, getting Grace to breastfeed, tugging on it, but it was anchored in place. At some point it was decided that it had to come out another way and they took Grace from my arms and gave her to Eddie, my rock. He'd made it to every prenatal appointment with the midwives, every childbirth education class at the Y, and learned how to help relieve my labor pain with a strong massage on my lower back until I finally pushed Grace out. We'd been dreaming of this moment—meeting our baby—from the first month we dated. Everything till now had gone to plan for the most part, until Grace was outside my body.

My midwife called the backing physician in. I was only supposed to see him again if there was an emergency. Was this an emergency?

The doctor told me he had to take the placenta out. He said, "It won't take long, but it's going to hurt." I barely comprehended his words, and certainly not the magnitude of them. There was no time for painkillers or mental preparation; I was losing blood. He reached his gloved hand inside. He wrenched and pulled on my placenta; it was embedded in the top inner wall of my uterus and he had to get every piece out. Leaving any fragments inside can lead to sepsis, a chain reaction in how your body reacts to infection. In severe sepsis, your organs can shut down, your blood pressure can fall dangerously low, and you can die.

Some ten harrowing minutes later, my placenta was out on the table. Medical science still doesn't know enough about how this mysterious organ works, and mine was no different. I lived to tell this story so many times—to other women who also survived it or other complications related to it, to conference rooms of doctors around the world, and to myself, as a reminder of how I met not only my baby girl for the first time but my purpose in life.

A retained placenta is when the placenta is not delivered within thirty minutes of the baby's birth. It is a serious problem since it can lead to severe infection or life-threatening blood loss. Retained placenta is not a common condition, but because it's serious, it must be managed by a medical team. After Grace's birth, I was on a mission to understand what had happened to me, and also how I could become useful as a result of it, in a spiritual sense. I spent the next few years traveling to Central and South America with CARE, one of the largest and oldest humanitarian organizations, learning about the disparities in global maternal health first-hand. My outcome could've been very different, I realized, if I'd given birth to Grace in a remote village in El Salvador, my mother's native country. My retained placenta didn't have dire consequences for me because of the great care provided by my birth team, but postpartum hemorrhage is one of the leading causes of maternal death in the world. Too many women don't have access to the high-quality care I received and either bleed out or die from infection. Once my eyes were opened to how lucky I was, I couldn't walk away and do nothing. In fact, I'd never see the world—or my role in it—the same way again.

Before we go further, let's back up to how most people know me first: as a model. When I started at fourteen, modeling was my passport out of boring suburbia and into New York City, or the Amalfi Coast, or wherever I was flying for a job that week. At first, my mom was constantly at my side but after a while, I didn't want her around anymore. I craved independence, so she returned to California to care for my two sisters. My agents were officially in charge of looking out for me, but let's be real, I was a teenager in New York City in the eighties. I'm still shocked sometimes that my parents agreed to this scenario so readily.

I wasn't thinking about getting pregnant, but I did sign some contracts when I was eighteen or nineteen and then another one at twenty-two, all of which had pregnancy clauses. The gist of those clauses was that they could immediately terminate the contract if I became pregnant. It gave me pause: Would I really lose my livelihood if I got pregnant? Looking back, those contracts feel unethical but I didn't know how to advocate for myself yet. By my midtwenties, I knew to cross out anything I didn't want. In the fashion world, like a lot of industries, once you have power you can exercise it.

By the time I met my husband, Eddie, I was in my early thirties and not modeling much at all. I had gone back to school, started a few businesses, and written a book. A few weeks into dating, we had settled on how many kids we wanted to have (four) and one of their names: Grace, after my grandmother. We couldn't agree on any other name, and we had three imaginary children to go. Regardless, we got engaged after five months.

Even before Grace's birth, Eddie and I were strapped in for a wild ride. We started planning our wedding for 2001—and then 9/11 happened. We canceled the wedding, and then we broke up. What can I say? The crisis really foregrounded some differences. My husband is from a blue-collar New York family, the son of a cop, and he took the perspective of **I could have been in there.** A kind of survivor's guilt haunted him. Meanwhile, my mother came to this country when she was eight and I grew up traveling the world, not defining myself as an American but something of a global citizen. We just didn't see the situation in the same way.

After six months apart, we came back together but things were touch and go. He was definitely a little guarded because I had encouraged our breakup. We were almost at a place where I was like, "Okay, if this isn't going to get better then forget it"—and that's when I got pregnant. We conceived at the Sundance Film Festival, where my husband's filmmaking career took off in 1995. He was back now as an actor and I came along for the ride. I could tell right away; I wasn't sick but I just felt very tired. Luckily, he was really happy when we found out. I was worried we'd have an "oh no" moment, but instead, it cemented our relationship.

After having some impersonal experiences at the doctor's office, I decided to go with a midwife, doula, and an unmedicated birth plan. Being a yogi, I trusted my body to handle physiological birth. I wanted to be present for the birth. Eddie was really supportive; he read pretty much every book. We also finally got married when I was twenty-five weeks pregnant at Saints Peter and Paul Church in San Francisco.

All was bliss until I was nearly two weeks past my due date. My doula asked me, "Why are you holding back? Why don't you want to have this baby?" First babies can take a long time to arrive. Our birth center had a rule at the time: If you went past two weeks, you had to deliver in the hospital. I still believe that hospitals are for sick people, not healthy ones. I didn't want to give birth in one, especially after my dad's death in 1997. Talking about his death, which I hadn't fully grieved, helped me prepare myself for birth. That, and seeing an acupuncturist and drinking castor oil.

Around midnight, labor started and before dawn, Amy, our doula, had arrived. Through the night, I climbed up and down the stairs, took lots of baths, and bounced on the birth ball. Maybe ten or eleven hours later, on the midwife's directive, we finally went to the birth center. By that point, I was in very intense labor pains. We drove up the West Side Highway, and I was slumped over the backseat with Amy massaging my lower back. I could see the city blocks as we were passing them, and Eddie kept saying, "We'll be right there!" And I was like, "Um, no, we're still twenty blocks away."

At the birth center, I labored back and forth between the bathtub and a double bed. In the bath,

I went from seven to ten centimeters. I knew by the sound of my voice that it was time, so I got out of the bath and onto a birthing stool to push.

At one point, Elizabeth, my midwife, said, "Here, you can feel your baby's head." I reached down to touch it and thought, **Shouldn't more be out? That's not enough head for me!** My husband was rubbing my back, but in that moment, my midwife was my person. We locked eyes. Out came the baby after just minutes of pushing. As soon as she was out, the pain was gone, all of it. Grace, our girl, was here at last. She came out with this serious expression—which is so revealing of her personality now. The sternness of this very new, very tiny person was unbelievably cute.

We graduated to the bed, where Amy encouraged her to latch on and nurse. Our playlist was still going and the energy in the room was so joyful. Adrenaline was running through my body like never before. She was born around four in the afternoon, less than two hours after I'd arrived.

Of course, that wasn't all the day had in store. Going through labor without meds was nothing compared to the manual extraction of my placenta. When I was laboring and even during the delivery, I was an active participant in the birthing process. But during the extraction, I was on my back and powerless in a way I had done everything I could to avoid. And I didn't understand: I'd seen my sister give birth to her daughter—wasn't delivering the placenta supposed to be the easy part? Why was this happening to me?

The aftermath brought its own trauma: To prevent a bacterial infection from the doctor's gloved hand, they had to give me antibiotics. I was so dehydrated and exhausted they could barely find a vein. I had a tear from pushing, which they closed with surgical glue. That didn't hurt, thank God, but they did have to catheterize me and that was painful too. The whole thing was **a lot.** What calmed me, finally, was having Grace back in my arms. She went right back to nursing.

Later that night, Eddie and Grace were asleep but I was wide awake with adrenaline. I could hear other women as they came into the birth center. I couldn't see them, but I could hear them as they got closer, recognizing those primordial sounds, and I would think, **Okay, I know which stage they're at right now.** When they would fall silent, I could vicariously feel that their baby was out. These women were strangers, but I was connected to all of them.

For the next several weeks, as Eddie and I learned how to pass the baby between us so the other one could eat or shower, I started to put the pieces together. In truth, there wasn't a clear explanation why my placenta grew into my uterine wall. Elizabeth assured me that the problem could not have been detected beforehand, and that I hadn't done something to bring it on. Not until I was pregnant with my second in 2006, nearly three years after Grace's birth, did I fully see how this experience had changed me in ways beyond the obvious. Becoming a mother was part of it, but I also discovered a deeper sense of purpose in my life.

My mom has long been involved with CARE, and when I was six months pregnant, we traveled with them to a village a couple of hours outside San Salvador to visit a clean water project. A lot of women had come on foot, pregnant, or with babies on their backs, incentivized to access clean water. While there, they could also receive basic antenatal health checkups in a place where they wouldn't otherwise have it available to them. If I had given birth to Grace in a community like this, where there was no clean water, no paved roads, where families lived in one-room tin-roofed houses, things would have played out very differently for us. In less than two hours, you can bleed to death from postpartum hemorrhage. After that trip, it was becoming clear to me: I would do all that I could to help other mothers survive pregnancy-related complications.

With our son Finn's birth, I had no complications, though he was a bigger baby and the birth happened much more quickly. I'd call him the "Double Ring of Fire": His head was one thing but his shoulders were another. Finn also had colic from four to twelve weeks, which made for a very bleak winter. Eddie and I were both sleep-deprived, which led to us arguing about how to manage in this state with a newborn and a toddler. I can only say that none of this seemed to rub off on Finn—he has the sweetest disposition.

The time I had at home with Finn allowed me to really plot my next steps. When he was about a year old, I traveled again with CARE to Peru and that further cemented what I wanted to do. We visited a community in the highlands, where CARE had worked with local government in partnership to reduce the high rate of maternal deaths in a very short period of time. It remains one of the best programs I've seen since. The program took into consideration the apprehension women felt about giving birth outside of their homes and addressed each of the identified barriers.

Some women came in from working in the field to deliver, standing fully clothed with a hat still on in the clinic. The medical team at the clinic had taken steps to make them feel comfortable and welcome. This included the use of floral sheets instead of hospital whites, and illustrations on the walls that showed the warning signs of certain complications, for those who couldn't read the words. They had written the names of women over the beds rather than numbers in the maternity ward. It was in the small details, the dignity and respect they tried to give the experience.

Back in New York, I told Eddie that I wanted to make a documentary about maternal health around the globe. Ever supportive, he encouraged me to reach out to a friend who made documentary films. From the time I came back from Peru onwards, I was on a course of action. I went back to school, with a two-year-old and four-year-old at home, at Columbia University's Mailman School of Public Health. I studied there for two years while I was making **No Woman, No Cry.** The film, completed in 2010, was a vehicle for my advocacy work and the true start of Every Mother Counts. Initially a campaign to support **No Woman, No Cry,** it quickly grew beyond that: In 2012, Every Mother Counts became a 501(c)(3). Now we've invested more than $21 million in twenty-nine programs across nine countries. I could never have imagined the impact we made in the first decade. But there's still so much more to do to address the inequities that exist here in the U.S. and around the world, inequities that are the root cause of most of these preventable maternal deaths.

Remember our fantasy about having four kids? Eddie and I let that one go, but whether to have a third child was definitely a sensitive topic for a while. After our second, Eddie was like, "We have a daughter and a son and they're both healthy; we're good." Eventually I agreed.

Finn is now sixteen and Grace will turn nineteen this year, old enough now for me to have gone through several different phases in my mothering journey. I'm not pining for when they were little because at every stage I've learned something new about myself and the world. I've learned how connected I am to other women, not just the ones in the birth center the night Grace was born but to every mother, everywhere. In the process of becoming a mother, I tapped into this larger sense of purpose that I couldn't have done any other way. The sense of discovery is one of the most exciting parts about motherhood: There is no way to know what's coming next, for them or yourself. It forces me to stay present, responsive.

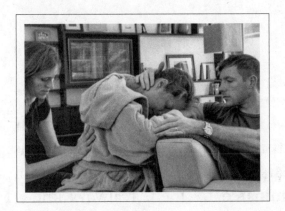

The Balance

EMILY OSTER

Professor of Economics

Before I became a mother, my job dictated everything in my life. I'm an economist and I've spent years working hard and proving myself in a field dominated by men. I always knew I wanted children, but I worried about how motherhood would affect my career, what I might have to give up at work in order to be a good mom, and what I might have to miss with my kids to perform and achieve professionally. I'm also pretty competitive and driven, and I wanted to "achieve" when it came to being a good mom the same way I did with my work.

Like my husband and me, my parents were also both economics professors at an Ivy League university. But it was my mother who was more involved in our day-to-day functioning, despite them both doing literally the same work. She picked up my two brothers and me from school, made our lunches in the morning, and got us to bed at night. When my husband, Jesse, and I were planning for our children, it became clear that I'd also be the "lead parent." Not in an unfair way—I wanted that involvement—but I was daunted by the challenge of balancing life as a present, engaged mom and a successful economist.

My husband and I got married right when I was finishing graduate school. It was time to lean into our careers, but we didn't want to put off having children for long. Luckily, we both ended up as assistant professors at the University of Chicago. Jesse got a tenured position very early and his job security allowed us to think about children sooner. With his job security in place, we tried to figure it out. But we were young and career-oriented, and neither of us quite knew how a baby would fit into our lives. A typical weekday for us was at the office; even a typical weekend day was spent at our computers, saying hi in the kitchen every few hours between research dives. We had no idea what it would be like to devote so much of our time to something else.

I knew my concerns about balancing work and motherhood were real and valid. In this male-dominated field, a lot of people, women in particular, drop out of research to have families. My job was so important to me, though. Quitting was never on the table. But I worried: **How am I going to keep building my career with babies in tow?**

I ended up merging the two—family and economics. When I was thirty, I stopped taking birth control and very quickly conceived. I was a little sick in the beginning but all in all, I had an easy time. I know I was very lucky. While I was pregnant, I became fascinated by all the choices to consider to supposedly maintain a healthy pregnancy. **Is it okay to drink wine in your second trimester, or to continue with your daily coffee habit?** I started writing my first book, **Expecting Better,** to help women navigate these choices using a data-driven approach. I was neck-deep in research for the book during my whole pregnancy. I taught in my second trimester and didn't stop going into the office until maybe the last week. I sold the manuscript for my book to a publisher at thirty-five weeks.

I planned on a traditional hospital birth with a doula present but I wanted to avoid an epidural. It can increase your recovery time (and sometimes your labor), but most of all, I wanted the challenge of going through birth on my own. I'm a runner, and I hoped I'd have the stamina to make it through unmedicated.

We labored at home with our doula until I was six centimeters dilated and then Jesse drove us to the hospital. The pushing wasn't going well for a while. The doctor held up a mirror down there and I could see her head starting to come out, then slipping back in, then coming back out, then slipping back in again. It was awful. Finally, she made it all the way out. They handed the baby to me, and Jesse and I were suddenly sobbing. I'd done so much research for my book, but none of it had prepared me for this feeling. It was more overwhelming than I expected, the sudden existence of this new person. There's a whole new person right here! Penelope Shapiro. One day Penelope is going to drive a car and have a job and well, everything else.

After that, it's a haze of the nurses bringing the baby to me, taking the baby, bringing her back, then I'm trying to feed her, and then at some point I realize I'm not wearing any clothes really and haven't for a long time. It was very bizarre, all of it.

Two days later, I drove us all home; physically, I was in reasonably good shape. But once we got home with her, we had no idea what to do. Normally, we'd maybe eat something and then go get some work done, but now there's this . . . **baby,** and the baby is just lying there sleeping. Obviously, I'm not going to go have a snack and tuck into my computer when my brand-new baby is right there . . . but then again, maybe I **should** do that? What else am I supposed to do while she's sleeping? And what happens when she wakes up and really wants something?

We fixated on solving whatever newborn problem cropped up that day or week. Every day fifteen boxes from Amazon arrived and yet, as my husband put it, "We are still undercapitalized," business-speak for when a company has insufficient resources to support its operation. We ordered new baby bottles, sleep sacks, video monitors, whatever we thought would help when Penelope was fussy or not sleeping or crying. Figuring out the needs of this person who could only communicate by crying was exhausting in a way I'd never imagined.

Our one real piece of foresight had been lining up a nanny before Penelope came. We were so lucky to have her, and I'm still grateful for all the ways she helped us. The nanny arrived very early in those days of chaotic uncertainty. She walked in, took a look at our Amazon-box-strewn house, and knew exactly what to do. She scooped up Penelope and said, "Okay, we're going on a walk." She buckled Penelope into the stroller and was out the door. We were blown away. We were like, "Oooh, you can take it out?"

Eventually we figured out enough things to muddle our way through that first year. Breastfeeding was particularly challenging. My milk took a long time to come in and in general, I didn't have that much supply. Penelope was pretty pissy about it. The logistics of pumping were also difficult. I constantly stressed over when to pump, how often, and what if she gets hungry while I'm pumping? Sometimes it seemed like my baby hated me and that just felt awful. Eventually I realized that I was breastfeeding because I felt pressured to achieve at it, and not because I valued its importance healthwise. I felt competitive with myself, and with other mothers who I felt were doing "better" than me because breastfeeding was easy for them. We ended up supplementing with formula, but it was really hard to recognize that I wasn't going to achieve breastfeeding in the way that I thought that I would.

By Penelope's third week, I started going back into the office. Maternity leave in the academic world has some significant ambiguity. In many ways, you set your own pace. But there is also a sense that people are watching you, keeping track of how hard you're seen to be working. I felt like I needed to prove I hadn't disappeared. At the time, my department had never tenured a woman with a child in the job that I had. I didn't want these guys to think, **Oh, you just had a kid and you've given up.** I tried to find silver linings to help myself get through that pressure, and I told myself that it was nice to get a break by going into the office, having a cup of coffee, and enjoying the company of other adults. But secretly, I wished I could've felt just as free to go to a coffee shop for all that instead of putting in an appearance at the office.

Looking back on it now, I'm more resentful of that implicit pressure to be seen doing my work. I certainly don't want junior people in my department now feeling the way that I did. Motherhood is work just the way being an economist is work, but that wasn't recognized. It's still not always recognized now. And in the end, none of my efforts mattered anyway because by the time Penelope was two and a half, I was turned down for tenure. Essentially, fired. What made it so painful, and partially why they passed on me, was that they didn't like my book, **Expecting Better.** The book was basically taking economics and putting it into your vagina. But not everyone was excited about this approach, or this choice of topic. Tenure decisions are always complicated; they're never just one thing. If I'd written more papers, better papers, this probably would have gone differently. But it was—and is—frustrating to feel that the book played a role. Nowadays, there are several books in the parenting-economic space. I admit, sometimes I catch myself thinking, **Great, but where were you when I was getting fired for this?**

It actually ended up working out for the best, because within a few months, Jesse and I both secured tenured positions at Brown, where we could be closer to our families. It was so exciting to have a place to land where we could be happy. Immediately, we started to try for our second kid. I pulled out the goalie (i.e., my IUD) and pretty quickly got pregnant again.

It's funny how much less momentous the second time was; when I found out, instead of waking Jesse up at 6:40 A.M. to tell him like last time—twenty whole minutes before our alarm, he griped—I sent him a Google Calendar invite for "Due Date." He accepted. We still laugh about that.

My second pregnancy was another easy ride, except for a hamstring injury around thirty-seven weeks. I couldn't walk very well after that, which I found frustrating. But it was indicative of the pregnancy at large. I was much less immersed in the experience, and much more on-the-go: We were new to Providence, new to Brown, I was teaching a new class, and Penelope was almost four years old. I wasn't willing to slow down on any of it. Parenting and work—I could do both.

At exactly thirty-nine weeks, I went into labor. I labored mostly at home, with the doula and Jesse by my side. Eventually we went to the hospital, where they had a laboring tub and a big bed, more of a birthing center setup. By the time we got there, I was eight centimeters dilated. I got in the tub for only a few minutes before I got out again and pushed him out. Barely twenty minutes after we'd arrived, Jesse and I curled up in the bed with Finn, our newest person, and fell asleep.

Penelope took to being a big sister right away. The person who struggled most with the transition to two kids was me. We had a structured life, and Finn fit into that very easily, but I missed my time with Penelope. Finn was a newborn and needed so much of my attention. Things settled, though, when they started to fall asleep around the same time; I could do bedtime with both of them, and not have to miss Penelope's. Suddenly, we were this complete family.

Having kids did change the direction of my career, but I'm not bothered by that. The change wasn't what I feared—that I'd get totally left behind—it just required me to cut my own path.

Having kids didn't become a distraction from my work, it became enmeshed with my career, the focus of so much of my research and, of course, my books.

Now Penelope is ten, and she's this very kind person with a tremendous imagination. Finn is six and crazy-silly and loves his friends. The older they get, the more I enjoy my kids. I still make sure to balance work and family, even in how I spend time with them. I make sure I spend time with them that isn't goal-oriented, that's not about homework or violin practice but just hanging out and being together. I want them to know that whoever they are is cool. I can already tell that it's very likely neither one of them will be an economist—and good for them! I can't wait to see who they will become.

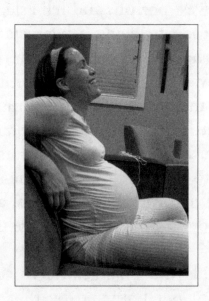

The Space Between Life and Death

EMMA HANSEN

Author and Model

I entered motherhood through grief. At thirty-nine weeks and six days pregnant with our first child, Reid, I woke up to find my womb had gone quiet. The kicks that often roused me from sleep had stopped and dread took over in their absence. My husband, Aaron, drove us to the hospital as I pressed gently on my belly and begged for movement. It was inside a dark room in Labor and Delivery that we heard the devastating words: "I'm so sorry, but your baby is dead."

It didn't occur to me that he still had to come out until I was told that I would have to birth him vaginally. The induction would start the next morning, so I was given a suppository to soften my cervix and sent home to rest. But labor began that evening, and continued strong and fast. We returned to the hospital, where I opted for an epidural. My water broke in a dramatic gush shortly after, and with one quick check I was told it was time, if I was ready. I started to breathe our baby down and out, fully aware of every movement despite the epidural, as I gently worked with each contraction. I felt an unexpected calm. Then finally, a few pushes later, relief.

Reid was born still on April 4, 2015. His death was caused by a true knot in his umbilical cord, a rare occurrence that happens in about 1.2 percent of all pregnancies and isn't usually fatal. We held him in our arms and memorized his features. Our families joined us in marveling over him. We gave him a bath and dressed him in his gray-and-white newborn outfit and had photos taken. We tried to create as many memories as we could in our fifteen hours together, and there were many beautiful ones. But no amount of time could have prepared us for saying goodbye. Years later, the echo of our mourning cries still rings in my ears.

A few days after Reid's birth, my milk came in. My body was providing for a child it didn't know was no longer there. It cried out for a way to nurture him. During pregnancy, you're called a mother-to-be, and after birth, with a living child in your arms, you are given the title of mother. But what are you when your baby has died? What are you when your experience is different from what is traditionally defined as motherhood? As a way to try to process his birth, and my identity as a mother, I started writing about my experience.

Sitting with my pain and sifting through the liminal reality of my present, I realized that my experience opened up the space between life and death. Slowly, from this gray place, I began to develop a language for my particular grief. This allowed me to stay close to my son, and to evolve my definition of motherhood. I began to comprehend you can't restrict it to a single description; motherhood is different for everyone. If you **feel** like a mother, you are.

I posted Reid's birth story, **Born Still but Still Born,** on my blog and immediately messages poured in. After a few days, the post went viral. I discovered how frequently these losses occur. Worldwide, 2.6 million families experience a third-trimester stillbirth annually. Even though that's what had happened to us, I was shocked when I learned that statistic. I felt so alone, but so many others were alone in the same way.

In 2020, on what would've been Reid's fifth birthday, I published **Still: A Memoir of Love, Loss, and Motherhood.** In the book, I wrote about Reid's death and birth but also what it felt like to balance hope, fear, and happiness after. Writing, revising, and sending the book out into the world over the course of five years was my way of mothering Reid, healing myself, and supporting others in their own experiences of loss.

Immediately after Reid's death, even right there in the hospital room, Aaron and I knew we wanted to have more children. The feeling was primal, a decision made for us. As my body went through all its postpartum motions—the slow and steady bleeding of a healing womb, the milk leaking from expectant breasts, the insomnia meant to mimic a newborn cycle—the possibility of creating and birthing new life that it could one day sustain became a sort of balm for the rawness of it all. Not an act of replacement but an act of hope.

The first year without Reid was marked by many painful anniversaries, reminders of what was supposed to have been. My grief manifested in my physical body as cycle disruptions, blood sugar issues, and postpartum thyroiditis. The journey to a second child involved medications and doctors' offices. I held pregnancy tests up against a flashlight, searching for any evidence of a positive result. Then one day, a little more than a year after Reid's death, I found myself staring at two pink lines.

It was here that I learned just how intertwined joy and sorrow are—how life after loss is full of experiences that hold seemingly opposing feelings in a single moment. Wanting to get pregnant and actually **being** pregnant again were two different things. I had already been the unlikely statistic once, and so I worried, what's to stop another bad thing from happening? Pregnancy after loss became a cyclical journey of travelling between a world full of trauma and worst-case scenarios, and a world of hope and dreams realized. It is one of the cruelest lessons in life: You can do everything possible and still not be able to keep your loved ones safe. I didn't have control over everything that might happen in this pregnancy. I relied heavily on the esteemed obstetrician I was privileged and grateful to receive care from. I learned to find comfort in the present moment. Literally, moment by moment. I would say to myself, "The baby is okay **right now**," and that would have to be enough. But mostly, I had to surrender to the unknowns.

The birth plan was to induce me at thirty-eight weeks, which was typical for a pregnancy after a late-term stillbirth. But at thirty-seven weeks and four days, contractions set in as Aaron and I walked around the neighborhood. They were strong enough to stop me in my tracks and force me to breathe through them, though I didn't believe I was in active labor. Suddenly, his movements changed. I contacted my OB, who suggested I go to the hospital to get checked.

In the car, the tightenings built in strength. In Admitting, the nurse gave me a nonstress test and it showed intense, regular contractions. By the time the OB came to check, I was nine centimeters dilated. I was raced to a birthing suite, down the same halls we'd staggered through with empty arms. In the room, I worked with the nitrous oxide I'd been offered to soften the pain. Each rush brought him closer to us. The moment I started to push was the moment I woke up. The grief, the numbness, the trauma that I met with Reid—I felt them burn with the fire that grew within me. Feeling everything allowed me to **feel everything**. Maybe this physical pain, which felt distant during Reid's birth, allowed me to embrace the emotional pain too. As his head emerged, the nurse asked if I wanted to touch him. I moved an unsteady hand downward and felt a soft skull and his slippery hair. One final push and our beautiful son, Everett, was born screaming.

Last time, only one beating heart. This time, two. Last time, I birthed my way into a new world of motherhood in the silence of my first child. This time, I became a different kind of mother in the roar of my second. When I pulled him up on my chest and felt his cries ripple through my body, the emotions poured into me, and I was transformed, again. There was a feeling like I'd been there before, but it was all new. He opened his eyes and looked at me—I held his gaze in that crowded room. Love felt like the only visitor. Love that travelled through time and beyond death to meet us in this moment we had longed for. This child was coming home.

In our apartment, anxiety consumed me. I couldn't bear to take my eyes off of Everett for more than thirty seconds, which is the amount of time they told us in a baby CPR class that an infant can turn blue from lack of oxygen. On our second day home, while we were preparing dinner, I glanced over at Everett, and saw his forehead was marbled, and his lips were inky blue. I screamed and picked him up, stripped him out of his swaddle, and furiously began to rub his back. He let out a cry and within seconds, he was no longer blue. Something still felt wrong, and we decided to take him to the hospital.

In the waiting room, he had another episode, much worse this time. A nurse ran our lifeless son down the hallway to the ER, and I lost sight of him as more nurses and doctors rushed in. But the image of his limp body had seared itself in my vision—he looked so similar to Reid. I was terrified that we had crossed the same threshold again. Everett was resuscitated and then intubated. We didn't know if he was going to be all right. We didn't know if this would continue to happen.

He got all manner of tests during his two-and-a-half-week stay at the NICU but we never got a firm answer about what happened. Eventually, the doctors decided that a virus he got at the hospital combined with sleep apnea created a perfect, horrible storm. He steadily improved in the hospital, and at some point, the doctors told us, we were going to have to believe that things would be okay. In the NICU, they instructed: "Don't look at the monitors, look at your baby."

Once we were home again, through every waking hour, we looked at him. That was the easy part. The hard part was looking away. We wondered how we were supposed to keep him safe without stifling him. That's parenthood though, isn't it? The continual return to a place that balances letting them live with keeping them alive. Still, even though he's now five years old, there are times when I wake up in the middle of the night and stand in his doorway and look over him, just to make sure that his chest is still moving, that he's still breathing. I don't know if there's ever going to be a point when I don't do that.

Every joyful new experience with Everett has been new for me too—the first time he laughed or rolled over or said mama. Of course, grief joined these milestones too. These are all the things that I imagined would happen while I was pregnant with Reid. In that first year after our loss, I ached with each celebration, thinking of the highlights Reid had missed. The pain also felt like gratitude; it kept me connected to my firstborn son.

We loved Everett more than we could grasp, and we also felt like our family was incomplete. On what would've been Reid's fourth birthday, we found out we were pregnant again with another boy. Their brotherhood expanded across three spheres; they were connected by more than just the home they shared in my body. At thirty-seven weeks, we induced. It was a decision led by an assessment of risks versus benefits and debilitating anxiety. During the last trimester he flipped between breech and cephalic dozens of times, so when an ultrasound a few days before showed that he had gone from head up to head down again, and that the cord was wrapped around his neck as a result, we had to weigh each option carefully. Nuchal cords are variations of normal. So are breech babies and true knots. And these variations are rarely problematic, let alone fatal. So was it necessary to panic? Did we need to intervene? We've had experience being the exception.

At seven centimeters my water broke and minutes later I found myself fully dilated and involuntarily pushing. Nurses searched frantically for a missing heartbeat, doctors were paged, and Aaron grasped my leg tightly. With the next contraction, as I bore down, I was told to stop. Instead of the crown of his head, the baby's nose and lips were coming out first.

On a cold late November evening in 2019, Atticus came out and from his brow to his chin, he was black-and-blue. Babies who are born face-first often have a lot of facial bruising from the way they are compressed as they exit the birth canal. Once again I was brought right back to after Reid was born, when his coloring changed from warm to cool in my arms. The doctor and nurses assured me that Atticus was just fine. I let out a huge breath of relief and held him close, basked in the love. Having such powerful flashbacks to Reid the first time I saw Atticus was a healing reminder that grief doesn't ever really leave; it becomes a part of your story, but it doesn't have to define it.

Everett and Atticus are kind and spirited. They differ in many delightful ways, but share a comedic desire to entice smiles from everyone they encounter. We don't know yet if our family is complete. It will always feel like someone is missing, because someone **is** missing. It's in the absences that I feel Reid most. It's everywhere that I had imagined he'd one day be. Each year, on April 4, rituals see us through. I beat cake batter by hand, sip a beverage, and sigh deeply to familiar songs. The kids point to Reid's framed photo and Everett asks a hundred questions that speak directly to my heart. Mostly, I remember. I remember what it felt like to rub the curve of my first baby's back through my belly. To hold his seven-pound, eleven-ounce body in the crook of my arm until it lost all sensation. To find that death, not life, would teach me how to mother.

Portions of this text were drawn from Emma's memoir, **Still: A Memoir of Love, Loss, and Motherhood** (Greystone Books, April 2020).

Matriarchy of Two
LESLIE FEIST
Musician

Adoption is a labyrinth; disorienting and confounding, but with a central quest. Once I'd found the way to my daughter, Tihui, on the other side, I could see that there was nothing about it that wasn't perfect. It was as if each roadblock had been the very thing designed to prepare me for the next and all of it, including the dead ends and self-doubt and night sweats, was exactly how it was supposed to have happened. Realizing the inevitability of this path to Tihui is as close to religion as I'll ever get, something experienced out beyond the scope of regular life. I felt it as an intensely private process likely because I was pursuing it on my own, and so, besides leaning hard on a few dear friends, I had to learn to keep my own counsel.

Most of my life the idea of kids was deep in my peripheral view, but if you'd have asked me, I would have assumed a person needed a partner to have a baby. Beyond the basic biological fact of it, maybe I imagined there would be safety in numbers and less responsibility on one person if it was undertaken by two. It may just have seemed that way to me as a child of divorce, growing up idealizing **Little House on the Prairie.** My mom left my dad just after I was born, and my older brother and I each had a shoelace with the house key around our necks from the time I was six. After we lived at our grandparents' for a few years, our little trio of my mom, my brother, and I were on our own until my brother moved to live with my dad when I was nine. From then on, my mom would wake me up for school by calling the house, having left for work at 5 A.M. I'd have to run the faucet within earshot of the phone to prove I was up and out of bed. There would be bread waiting in the toaster next to the peanut butter jar, or an omelette in the pan, and I'd lock up and go to school.

I should've had so much admiration for my mom—and now, of course, I understand better what she was managing—but in my own early relationships, being a single mom felt like a cautionary tale to be avoided at all costs. In my twenties, I was determined not to let it happen to me, and yet growing up in our household didn't teach me any skills to avoid it. I was in a few serious relationships throughout my twenties and thirties, either feeling like I was building something new or working to avoid something old. I figured kids would just happen at some point, imagined in a soft lens wholly serving romance, but in retrospect I really was mostly focused on my work.

When my album **Let It Die** came out in 2004, I found new ears had opened to what I was doing. Working in relative obscurity, zigzagging North America and Europe on tour from the age of fifteen, had primed me to respond by working doubly hard. I used to joke I was a Clydesdale, just head down and pulling my weight, plus whatever weight was hitched to me. My manager would say, "Thirty-year-old Leslie is working this hard for forty-year-old Leslie. She'll thank you one day." Which of course has proven true.

For probably six or seven years, over the span of **Let It Die** and then **The Reminder**, I was touring ten or eleven months a year. At some point some wise and tired part of me drew a line in the calendar and made a hard stop, desperate to learn to stay still. I had a kind of velocity fatigue, couldn't stand to watch the world whip by from a plane or car or train window anymore. I rented a little house covered in ivy, planted tomatoes, bought a bike, and hung laundry on the line. Doing anything I could to feel domestic, I tried and failed and tried again in a kind of needlepoint embroidery—just a tableau of what I was hoping I'd find. In among bonfire night swims in lakes and reading Wendell Berry, I wrote

Metals and then started touring again in 2011. Touring can be a strangely wonderful way to spend your time when curiosity is intact and energy is high, but everything in moderation. It can also be a wind tunnel, blotting out the sun, skewing priorities, grinding down the warmth of simple routine and replacing it with adrenaline-laced repetition. Each time I'd step out from the tunnel, especially the last time, I found that my friends were shape-shifting into adults, buying houses and having kids. It started to feel like there were two paths: One was high-effort beach picnics and couch forts and the other was a kind of never-ending golden-hour dinner party. I felt a slow pivot from one foot to the other, but felt like I ultimately belonged on team sock puppet. The puttering grilled cheese maker in me was deeply unsatisfied and my freedom was giving me vertigo, a feeling it took a long time to name.

The decision to become a mom on my own was a hard one, and as intentional as adoption has to be, I was still backing in, trying to avoid the reality of it. As I struggled with my growing pains and rode through waves of doubt and pessimism, a single mother and dear friend of mine advised, "Don't look for feelings yet, just keep pushing past the paperwork and the feelings will come when it's time. Trust yourself!" During the litany of background checks and bureaucratic tangles, I had plenty of opportunity to consider my motivations and what was driving me toward building a life with a child.

It was very slow and sad, this reckoning which was simplified, painfully, by the practical; I had just turned forty and didn't want to bring a baby into a new and unknown relationship, or ask my body to do something it didn't seem inclined to do. Such a stark assessment, once it truly sank in, gave me a sense of purpose much bigger than any relationship had ever offered me.

The first challenge of adoption, no matter if it's international or domestic, undertaken on your own or in a couple, is finding trustworthy people to guide you through the process. I couldn't find anyone to draw me a map, but had one fateful meeting with an adoption counsellor in Canada, where I grew up, that led me to understand I may have a better chance if I went through the process with my American citizenship, in the States. I knew Los Angeles well and had lived there in between tours for years, so it seemed like the natural place to settle. There was a long period where I talked to all sorts of people— friends of friends, say, who would steer me towards a certain agency, but I'd either get cold feet after an orientation, or in one case, the agency I'd chosen to move ahead with ended up closing under a cloud of controversy. It felt too high stakes to be guessing, but that's what I was doing until I found my social workers.

On a friend's recommendation, I found Vista Del Mar Child and Family Services, the oldest adoption agency in California, with adoption being just one arm of their community services. From the first meeting with the director, I felt at ease. She wasn't trying to sell me a damn thing and I felt comfortable and supported. She recommended a long-respected and trustworthy lawyer who could connect me with birth parents looking to place a child, warning me that after forty years of liaising adoptions, he was a bit of a curmudgeon. Vista Del Mar would conduct my home study and be there to hold my hand through the process as my advocates and advisors. I finally felt I had found the right allies to walk me through the maze.

I completed my home study, which took about six months and helped me undergo a kind of mental gestation, transforming my daydreaming into a daily list of tasks to complete—which I guess is parenting in a nutshell. Over the next six months or so, the lawyer presented me with two potential matches, but no part of me felt that these options were meant for me. I turned them down, which caused me some doubt but was also a kind of commitment to my intuition. In the light of Tihui and I being together now, I know exactly what bone-deep sense of rightness I was waiting to feel. A central lesson adoption taught me over and over was to trust the ineffable as much as the facts.

I went back on tour and shared with my managers that at any point I could get a call and have to leave. I'd been told it could take anywhere from six months to two years after completing the home study to find a match, so the whole thing felt like a translucent mirage I was still very far from. Yet it was only a few weeks later, on a flight from New York to Los Angeles, while above Nevada, that I got another email from the lawyer. I told myself to wait until I got home to read it without any distractions, but the first moment I was alone, in the baggage area at Burbank airport, I read through the PDF he'd included from a young birth mother, in Nevada. Her answers to these basic form questions showed her sense of self and strength of character. Reading it, I felt an inexplicably deep recognition, like this was who I'd been waiting to hear from. For one, she was pregnant with a girl and I'd had a very powerful dream, likely part of why I trusted my determination to make this family, of my daughter coming to me and telling me her name. And this little girl was arriving in two short weeks, which had also been a quiet dream of mine: to be matched with a birth mother further along in her pregnancy and therefore, I felt, farther along in the certainty of her choice. The baggage carousel was the first of many places I'd cry in overwhelm and awe at the serendipity of this story unfolding. I was told by the lawyer to write the birth mother a letter that night and had absolutely no idea what to say. Things had shifted from an abstract pursuit to the high stakes of conveying my feelings to a young woman I didn't know a thing about. I didn't want to be presumptuous or say too much or not enough—but an adoptive dad friend gave me some advice from his own experience facing the same task: "Just write from the heart. You are equals and equally vulnerable here. Just tell her how you feel."

A few days later, back on tour, I was at a bar with friends on a night off in New York when the lawyer called. I paced the side streets of Brooklyn while he told me the birth mother had chosen me from the other prospective parents, and I was welcome to come to the birth, which would be in Nevada. I hung up from the call and stared up at the night sky, cherishing this liminal state from between parked cars. I wiped the tears off my face, slapped my cheeks red again, and went back inside holding the news quiet in my heart. I had a few more shows to finish out the tour, and my instincts, with a few exceptions, were to guard this news from my band and crew, if only to safeguard the rarefied air of these last days before my life would be so utterly changing. I played those last shows floating twenty feet above my body, simultaneously saying goodbye to an entire life I'd built and feeling my strength and capacity to build a new one on its foundation. Everything was shifting and I felt a light-headed thrill to be moving so unambiguously toward my intention to offer myself as a mother to this child.

I moved out to the desert to wait for the birth mother to go into labor. I'd shared the news with my closest friends and felt the village gathering. A care package was waiting for me on the front steps of my rental house from Tyler, the first of my friends to become a mom years ago. My dear friend Ariel flew in to distract me with day margaritas and pawnshop visits, which we later joked was my baby shower. And then Daniela came in to be with me, guiding me through meditation to prepare and center myself. I was never alone; it was incredible how quickly my community rallied around me, gently shaking me from my stunned stupor and giving me the context of chosen family. Their arrivals and departures dovetailed in a way they literally couldn't have planned.

I had told the social worker that I was available for anything the birth mom may want or need, whether that was something simple or even to just give her some space. Even now I feel her name isn't mine to share and if she were ever to read this, I'd just want her to recognize this story as true and feel the respect I have for her. The night she was due, she reached out through the social worker and asked if I'd like to go for dinner. I was so relieved I'd have a chance to spend some time with her and not be meeting in the delivery room. She was lovely and bright-eyed, forthcoming and self-possessed. We relaxed into talking about our lives in broad strokes and I noted small things like how kind she was to the waitress. I had no doubt she would make a determined and dedicated mother, but as she told me, as soon as she learned she was pregnant she knew she wanted this child to live a different life than the one she had experienced growing up. She suffered the indignity of systemic familial poverty but had dreams of going to school, getting a good job, and of offering support to the family she already had. I felt humbled by how resourceful, tough, and tender she was, and how hard her life sounded to have been. She told her story without a trace of self-pity and I felt humbled recalling my own lamenting over the years for such comparably small problems. Despite our age difference and wildly different lives, I felt us sitting there as equals who felt equally grateful for the role we were playing in each other's future. I told her that she was changing my life and that she could trust me to give this girl everything she'd need to thrive.

The next day she went into labor. My old friend Adrienne, a psychotherapist and single mother, was now at my side; her plane had landed just as the labor began. She said, "Don't ask her what she needs, just try to intuit it." I had brought lemon wedges for her, after seeing how much she craved them at dinner, and ice cubes to suck on. In between contractions she joked and chatted about everything from UFOs to wondering what Canada was like. The nurse, who was in and out of the room many times, said that we were the friendliest birth mother and adoptive mother pair that she'd ever seen. She herself had adopted two daughters and while guiding the birth mom through her labor, told us her own story. Despite a few moments of unkind treatment from a couple doctors, to which she responded with a grace and patience I don't think I could have managed in her place, the labor was going well. The nurse was talking to us about her daughters when suddenly the monitors began a frenzy of beeping and she left the room mid-sentence. A moment later, there were seven people surrounding us saying that the baby needed to come out now. No one was telling the birth mom or me what was going on and she began to ride the wave of another contraction. I learned later that the baby's heart rate had dropped drastically, and so very quickly the nurses helped her push and I stood in awe while Tihui's head appeared. Even as Tihui was crowning, this remarkable young woman stopped pushing and with clear eyes and a calm voice, reiterated that she wanted me to cut the cord and for the baby to go to me first. As she had told me at dinner, it was important to her that this little girl immediately feel a bond with the woman who would be her mother, a declaration I admired as a tangible act of her love and certainty. Tihui would be double loved from the moment of her birth. I had tears streaming down my face, in awe of this strong and generous young woman and of this moment that a friend had called "stardust come earthside." The moment a new life arrives.

Tihui came out looking in my direction with a shock of thick black hair and the umbilical cord wrapped around her neck three times. They twirled her around until it was unraveled and she let out a loud wail that I'm sure I'll remember for the rest of my life. Instantly, I was hit with a feeling that I had seen her before, which was echoed by my dad a few days later when he said, "Why does she look so familiar?" I knew he meant that in a way much deeper than her appearance. The familiarity made no sense to me, but it was undeniable that she was the little girl with the dark hair from my dream. It was the most wild and visceral moment of my life; the room full of such focused intensity, her birth mom smiling and clearly so relieved, while I did as she had asked and cut the cord connecting them.

After they checked Tihui out under the bright lights, they placed her on my chest for skin to skin while the birth mom looked on and chattered excitedly about how strong she looked. I was wearing a gold necklace with charms from my grandmother's charm bracelet, one of which is my own birth announcement on a little baby silhouette. Tihui reached up for those dangling charms and clutched them with an iron grip. I have some beautiful photos of this first contact, her determination and strength in clinging on to that necklace and blinking up with these massive almond eyes. She had joined the lineage. I still wear that necklace, and now there's another charm on it with Tihui's birth announcement. One day, it will be hers, along with our story.

For the first few hours, we were all in the same hospital room. Adrienne helped us maintain a warm and boundaried atmosphere, but to be honest that wasn't hard. There was a very easy and natural warmth in the room, all of us equally marvelling at Tihui. After being discharged, I spent a couple weeks of gentle desert day-nights learning the rhythms of this new little being, and then Mia came, the last of Tihui's new aunties, to drive us across the desert and home. The birth mom told me later that her milk hadn't come in, which seemed almost symbolic of how clear she was in her choice. She still checks in from time to time with thoughtful and enthusiastic texts and I follow her lead as to how much contact I sense she wants. I have no doubt that with time, we'll find a way to grow into friends and I hope Tihui will have a chance to know this remarkable woman.

Tihui is part-Latina and part-Caucasian. I named her Tihui after a friend in Mexico City, a woman whose warmth and magnetism is immediate and who tells fantastic stories. One of the first ones she ever told me, over a beautiful lunch made by her husband, Claudio, was about her name. Her parents took it from the indigenous Nahuatl language, spoken by the Aztecs, and it's the name for a mythological bird who sang, "Tihui! Tihui!" which means, "Follow me, I know where we're going!" And I feel she does! I'll be trying to keep up with her for the rest of my life, she's so strong and happy and determined. At twenty months, she's got her own vocabulary, a syllable for everything and infectious excitement that makes people smile on the street.

She's unstoppable and I feel her just gathering strength like a beautiful storm.

My friend Cass once said to me that a kid will incinerate you. As her single friend contemplating raising a child alone, I thought that sounded awful but she explained: A child will incinerate you and then whoever you are when you rise from the ashes is a much more interesting person to be for the rest of your life. For the first few months at home with Tihui, I was burned to a crisp. My friend and nanny, Caely, along with her girlfriend, Sara, supported me for almost a year. As they say, it takes a village. We made an unlikely pod through the pandemic and lived in the Canadian countryside, the needlepoint tableau now a hive of activity. I was bleary-eyed, could barely think straight, and the meaning of an hour, especially an hour of stolen sleep, totally changed. My whole internal scaffolding had to be rebuilt. The distance from one side of the house to another shifted as I gave myself permission to stray for a minute, and then leave the house for an hour, and eventually to leave for the afternoon. Distance and time changed, with Tihui as my new centrifuge. There was also so much gratitude and when I'd had enough sleep to think clearly, I felt relief to relinquish my spot as the center of the universe. That relinquishing has been the first step into becoming the person I'm much more interested in being for the rest of my life.

I've been hesitant to share the story of how Tihui

came to be my daughter. As her mother, I'm protective, but mostly I'm aware that this story isn't only mine to tell; it's the collective story of her and me and her remarkable birth mother. Nothing bigger has ever happened in my life, and I'm still so protective of it, but I feel strongly that if I tell it honestly, maybe it could serve people facing their own lonely questions. When I started thinking about adoption, I didn't have any mentors who had taken this path and it was hard to find other women who hadn't taken the more traditional routes we all grew up assuming are "normal." Now Tihui and I have built a little matriarchy of two, and I hope we can bust some assumptions down the line. I want anyone facing this same question to feel empowered and entitled to a whole color wheel of decisions. If adoption is right for you, nothing will be more humbling or empowering.

An Exchange of Breath
DR. AMANDA WILLIAMS
OB-GYN

I wanted to be a doctor long before I can recall wanting children. Motherhood was a daunting proposition for me. Even as a young child, I was much more comfortable professing my career goals than imagining myself fumbling over a baby.

My parents were towering examples of professional success. Throughout my childhood, they worked at big corporate law firms in Washington, D.C. My mother was the first Black woman partner in her firm, and my father was the second Black partner in his firm. It was the eighties and they had to prove that they were hot shit to these white boys by working their tails off. I admired them tremendously, but because their careers were so demanding, my two younger brothers and I didn't get a lot of their presence or nurturing as kids.

My paternal grandparents lived very close by, and they were hugely present in our lives, especially my grandmother Mumsie. She was my best friend in the whole world. My brothers had each other, and my grandmother and I would play together. Mumsie was no slouch in the professional department either: She had a doctorate in early childhood education, which was exceedingly rare for a Black woman born before 1920. My maternal grandmother was also on the scene, offering cool, sassy takes over her daily glass of white wine, which was my job to fetch. But it was Mumsie who was my idol, and, in many ways, she fulfilled the traditional motherly role in my life.

Karen, my mother, gave me an acute sense of what it meant to fight for your place as a female Black professional: Black and female, she'd say, those are two strikes against you. You'll have to work twice as hard to go half as far. She set the tone for the household, which viewed the world without much emotion, in very black-and-white terms. But she didn't really impress upon me what it meant to be a mother. I grew up wishing we were closer. Did she really love and see me, Amanda, or did she just care about my GPA? I felt a longing to be truly **seen** by her, and vice versa, all my life. This longing, it's painful to say, will never be fulfilled. She developed dementia in her early sixties and now, in the advanced stages, she's become a shadow of her former self.

Eventually, I did become a mother, twice over, and it was Mumsie who bore her influence over me, and over my first birth in particular. While I was growing up, my grandmother was energetic and strong, but she'd always say, "I gotta stay healthy to see Amanda's baby." It was like a mantra for her. Her own past with pregnancy would come to weigh on mine: Back in the forties, she was pregnant and diagnosed with preeclampsia, called "toxemia" back then, and almost died from a stroke. Tragically, she lost her baby. She wanted me to get pregnant, but it was also a terrifying prospect for her; that history would repeat itself.

After I graduated from Harvard, I went to Emory for my M.D. and my master's in public health. Near the end of my time there, I met DeAndre, my husband. I let him know right away that I was in no rush to have children, but I was quite intrigued by his enthusiasm for it. He seemed like he'd be a great father, which was reassuring because secretly, or not so secretly, I was worried that I wouldn't be such a great mom. His confidence, and his promise that he'd be the primary caretaker, really helped me ease into the idea. That, and my med school mentor told me that there's no good time to have a baby in your career, so you may as well go for it whenever you're ready.

There was a fork in the road at the end of my third year in residency: I could either be a generalist ob-gyn or I could train in a subspecialty like gynecological oncology. The latter was tempting; I loved being in the operating room, but I decided to let my body make the call. I stopped my birth control and said I'd give it three months. If I got pregnant, then I'd stick with being a generalist; if not, I'd move on to oncology.

The universe spoke clearly: I got pregnant right away. The generalist path wasn't particularly easy; I worked eighty-hour weeks delivering babies, performing six-hour-long operations, but I wasn't that concerned. I had just turned thirty. I was young and healthy, a former Division I athlete who competed in a half marathon during my second trimester.

With her granddaughter now pregnant, Mumsie changed her mantra. It went from "I gotta stay healthy to see Amanda's baby" to "I gotta be here to teach Amanda's baby how to read," a fitting promise from an education specialist. I was grateful because now that I was expecting a baby soon, I wanted her around as long as possible!

At this point in my training, I learned more about the disparity in health outcomes for Black women compared to their white peers. I learned about some of the historical atrocities in gynecological treatment for women of color, stories like James Marion Sims, "the father of gynecology," who performed painful, experimental surgeries on female slaves in the antebellum South under the commonly held belief that Black people didn't feel as much pain (a perception that lingers to this day). All of this knowledge has driven me to take the mentoring of fellow Black women in my field very seriously so we can work to actively change the way the medical profession sees and treats people of color. All that said, I was still blind in many ways to my own illness when pregnant, largely due to internalized racism.

I deliberately didn't immerse myself in the pregnancy experience as a form of self-protection. I knew from my work that women who get attached to a particular pregnancy or birth experience are really disappointed when the plan deviates, which it almost always does. And my pregnancy was quite easy—barely any morning sickness, no back pain or anything—until the very end.

At about thirty-five weeks pregnant, as the chief resident in OB-GYN at UCSF, I was on my feet yet again for a long surgery, and one of my colleagues noticed that my feet were very swollen. Within twenty-four hours, I was diagnosed with preeclampsia. It wasn't exactly a surprise—I had borderline hypertension, a history of preeclampsia in my family, and I'm a Black woman having her first baby, all risk factors. After a few days at home, I'm embarrassed to say that I didn't catch one of the cardinal signs that my condition was worsening. I called one of my colleagues to report that my vision was blurry, probably, I thought, because I was watching more TV than ever with all my newfound time off.

At my colleague's urging, I came in for more tests, and it was clear I needed to get induced immediately. At thirty-five and a half weeks, I was not ready. There was such a disconnect for me: **How did**

I go from being the healthy, young pregnant doctor with no discomfort to the severe preeclampsia patient so fast?

I was induced at the hospital where I was doing my residency, UCSF. In the beginning, the induction was like a tailgate party; we had coolers with drinks, doctors and nurses coming in and out, and the Giants game on TV because my husband is a fan. My mother was there too, and Mumsie, my father, and my brothers were on their way. Then it got more serious: I insisted on laboring in the bathtub because I'm a water person. A big risk when you have preeclampsia is having a seizure, so normally a bathtub would be off-limits, but I signed an against medical advice form and got in. Not long after, I was completely dilated. In twenty minutes, I pushed out my first son, William, around 3 A.M. He was pale, but had so much sass. I huddled with him in the bed, breathless but thrilled that he had come out so fast. He looked at me like, **Are you ready, lady?**

We called Mumsie so that she could hear William's cry over the phone. That was a spectacular moment; she was just **so** happy. The nurse carried William over to the warmer for tests, and I dozed off for a couple of hours.

When I woke up, he was gone. The nurse told me he was in the NICU because he'd been grunting and not breathing well. I tried not to panic—he was a bit premature, after all—and I fell back asleep for another hour. When I woke up, they told me that he'd gotten worse. He might need to be intubated, the nurse said, and my blood turned to ice. I was on a magnesium drip and could barely walk or think straight. My husband went down to check on him.

That evening, from a wheelchair, I saw baby William and all his equipment in the NICU. I was in shock. At thirty-five weeks, only 10 percent of babies have respiratory distress; I didn't think it would happen to us. I went back to my room to sleep, devastated, but hoping he'd be better by the time more members of our family arrived the next day.

Overnight, William was intubated. In the morning, finally able to walk again, I visited him in the NICU. Everyone was being strange with me, very quiet. Finally, my brother told me what everyone had been holding back: "Amanda," he said, "Mumsie is dead." I said, "What are you talking about? She's on a flight out here right now." "No, she had a massive stroke in the morning before she got on the plane and died." Then the rest of my family filed into the hospital room, in tears. My father, this man who never showed much emotion, was sobbing like I'd never seen, full-bodied heaving. I started screaming. I can't remember a time in my life when I was as overwhelmed and grief-stricken as that moment. My grandmother, my best friend who I'd just talked to hours before, had dropped dead. And my baby was intubated. The world was crashing around me.

Women who have severe preeclampsia have a higher chance of high blood pressure and stroke later in life, and Mumsie had already had a few small strokes. But it's like she predicted this exchange of breath between her and William all my life. Later that morning, William improved and was extubated, medical-speak for he had his breathing tube taken out. In our family, we say that Mumsie gave her last breath to William. God exchanged one beacon of unconditional love in my life for another.

William was in the NICU for ten days, the hardest days of my life. I couldn't go to Mumsie's funeral because of William's fragile condition. When I went back to work a month or so later—the rules around a resident's absence at the time prohibited me from taking more time off—I was a zombie. Depression has affected me on and off since I was a teenager, but this was like nothing else. The sleeplessness from having a newborn mixed with the deepest grief hung like a thick fog between myself and anyone I tried to talk to, patients included. My directors sent me home; I arranged to finish some of my work after graduation.

I was able to attend my grandmother's memorial service and interment, about a month later. Eventually, I resumed work, but it wasn't easy. I was pumping all the time, which is the sort of difficult labor people don't credit nearly enough. I had to sit in the car or hide in the bathroom several times a day. Later in my career, when I became a manager, I made sure our physicians could get the time and space they needed to pump and breastfeed because it never happened for me.

Around eleven months after William was born, I

was able to take time off and really enjoy him. That marked a huge transition for me, a path back to the living. My second son, born a couple of years later, was a totally different experience.

Once again, I enjoyed an easy pregnancy after conceiving the same month I pulled out my IUD. (Note to patients: Your body does **not** need time to reset, so don't stop birth control till you're ready!) A few days before my due date, with preeclampsia nowhere in sight but still an all-too-real specter, I decided to induce again. This time, I hung a sign on the door: "Having a home birth in the hospital." I covered all the monitors. I wouldn't let any nurses or doctors in. Just me, my husband, and my doula. No medication. Though Sam was a big fat baby at almost nine pounds, he came out after just two pushes. He was the most cuddly teddy bear with huge cheeks.

I went hiking in the hills every day with Sam strapped onto my chest. I basically carried him around for two years, the whole attachment parenting routine, while running after William. I still worried that Sam wasn't getting enough direct engagement from me, because my attention was divided, but he's such a well-bonded child. It's a great lesson in parenting; sometimes you don't have to do as much as you think you do. The basics of snuggling and breast milk are incredibly powerful.

Looking back on it all now, both my medical practice and my purpose in life feel tremendously rich because of what I went through as a mother. I know that I'm here on this planet to raise these two boys to be great citizens of the world, and to take care of women of color, in particular, in this maternal health space. I'm also here to seek joy for myself, to be content and fulfilled.

William is now a sixteen-year-old Black boy who's more than three times likely to die at the hands of the police than his white counterparts. Sam is fourteen. No cop is going to ask about the fancy private school they attend, or what their grades are; they beat people up first, and ask questions later.

I'm having the conversations about the impact of racism nearly every day, at home and at work. I lived it as a pregnant person: I didn't listen to my own body when I had this terrible illness, and I'm an ob-gyn trained at arguably the premier program in the entire country. So, if I couldn't see it myself, what's it like for all the other Black women in America who don't have as much privilege? Doing what I can to advocate for these women, and my sons, is the passion that drives every single day.

A New Identity
ANGEL GEDEN
Inclusion and Diversity Program Manager

At age twenty-five, I told my then husband, Rob, that my biological clock was ticking. Looking back, I have to laugh. Of course I had plenty of time, but I just couldn't wait to become a mother. Motherhood was an identity that couldn't be questioned, which appealed to me because I'd been questioning my identity my whole life. I wanted to be an honest and authentic mother who would raise my children with more confidence than I'd ever had.

I grew up in a mostly white, working-class neighborhood in Chicago, and I never felt like I fit in. I was asked, "What are you?" on nearly a daily basis. I'm from many different backgrounds—my mother is second-generation Polish and my biological father, born in Chile, is a mix of Native

American, Spanish, Portuguese, West African, and Norwegian. To be a multiracial child back then who presented as more Latinx than white left me feeling like I didn't belong anywhere, like I had no certainty in my own identity, especially since I didn't speak Spanish. Even before I became a mother, I knew I wanted my children to grow up feeling completely confident in who they were and to never question their ancestral roots.

After my parents divorced, I lost touch with my biological father, and my mother remarried a great guy named Joe Geden. They had my two youngest sisters, who are also fair. Joe became Dad to me, and to this day, we have such an easy, joyful relationship. If I'm down, Dad can make me laugh and feel better in two minutes.

When I went to college at Northwestern, located in Evanston, one of Chicago's more diverse suburbs, I navigated my identity on my own for the first time. Without my mom, dad, or my sisters around to define me as white, if only by proxy, I felt adrift. But I also started to feel liberated to figure out my identity for myself. Without my biological father around to help me define what it means to be Chilean, I had to discover for myself what was in my DNA. I had to navigate my identity at a time when there wasn't 23andMe or Ancestry.com. My extended family can be racist and narrow-minded; their viewpoints had me believing I was white and only white, that I could improve my social acceptance with a white partner, that I was better off without whatever being Chilean meant for me. On my own, I had a chance to form friendships and relationships with people from many different cultures and backgrounds. I dated people who didn't look like me, mostly Black men, and that felt freeing. For the first time, with Black friends and Black partners, I felt like I belonged. I might not have known my exact genetic DNA at the time, but my soul knew it had found family.

My first husband, Rob, is Black. He rose up from a tough childhood where he experienced poverty to become a computer lab tech at school. Everyone in the community knew and loved him. I liked that he knew how to survive and provide, no matter what. Being with Rob also helped me figure out myself, in a way. With him, I could be a proud woman of color. Together we could make a family that celebrated all aspects of our backgrounds.

After I told Rob that my biological clock was ticking, it took about four months to get pregnant. At that age, it felt like a grueling eternity. When we finally got pregnant, I was so excited to share the news with my mom. But she said something hurtful and racist that really messed with my head: "Well, now you're stuck with Rob." I told her I didn't understand. She continued: "You're going to have Black children, so no white man will ever marry you."

I let my mom's comment slide, but I was shocked and hurt. It was a horrible thing to say. I was still so young, and my identity was still in flux. I knew what she'd said was morally wrong and also logically incorrect. It made me question my identity and my worth as a mixed human being. Had I done something wrong?

The worries that crept in after my mother's comment faded from my mind after a while, and I focused on my pregnancy. I wanted a beautiful, unmedicated birth—lavender candles, meditation music playing, etc. At thirty-seven weeks, the doctors told me he was breech, and my plans for my Mother Nature birth went out the window. They offered to do a version, which is when they try to turn the baby around using pressure on the outside, but it can end with complications, including the death of the child. Those risks, while admittedly low, didn't sound worth it to me.

We scheduled a C-section for a week before his due date, but he decided to come sooner. A few days before the C-section, I started to feel very off while walking through the grocery store. I had no idea whether I was in labor or not. My mom, a pediatric nurse, urged me to go to the hospital and so did my younger sister, a mother of two already, who came with me. The hospital thought I was having Braxton Hicks contractions due to dehydration, so they pumped me full of IV fluids. Then they wanted to send me home, but my sister, who knows how to be pushy, wouldn't let them. They agreed to monitor me for another thirty minutes. Finally, they concurred: I was in labor.

They gave me meds for the C-section, but I had eaten earlier in the day (you're supposed to have an empty stomach). I was miserable, completely out of it, and throwing up. When Joey was born, I remember seeing him for a blurry moment and that's it. The next morning, I properly met my son, named after my dad. I instantly knew him. I had sensed his personality already from his movements in the womb, and now he was outside of me. That was the hardest part to accept: My greatest happiness, my heart, lived outside of me now. How would I ever survive if anything happened to him?

Once we got home, I dove headfirst into my new role as mother. There's no other role that I have felt so born to do. Finally, my identity and purpose snapped into focus. For my whole life before being a mother, my sense of identity had been ever shifting. But holding Joey, I felt something inside me align, and it gave me a sense of who I was, at my core. Still, I made some rookie mistakes: Once, when I fell asleep breastfeeding him, I woke up to my baby crying on the floor. I had accidentally pushed him out of the futon. I was terrified. It was a sign that I wasn't sleeping enough or getting enough to eat.

Rob was raised by a strong single mother and

expected that I would be the one to handle everything for our child too. In his eyes, I would take care of Joey because that's what Rob saw as the glue of his community: strong mothers. But that left Rob without a parenting role. All the decisions around childcare fell to me. If I wanted to do something, I had to ask Rob to "babysit," as he called it. I'd grown up most of my life with a dad who was hands-on and involved. I didn't want Rob to sit in the living room drinking beer while I cooked dinner. We either had to shift the family dynamic, or it was going to fall apart.

Like a lot of young couples, we thought we could fix our marriage by having another child. We bought a house the same week I learned I was expecting our second baby. That pregnancy was tough; I got huge very quickly and had a toddler to chase. I'd lock myself in the bathroom and cry all the time, overwhelmed by my failing marriage and the idea of bringing another little human into it.

My C-section went smoothly, to my relief. After Eddie was born, I focused on getting out of the hospital right away. I just wanted to be with my babies, but now I wonder **why** they let me go so immediately without any questions. No one at the hospital thought to ask, "Are you okay? Do you need any support?"

At home, I sunk into a deep depression, and I was diagnosed with postpartum depression. My marriage was worse than ever. The only place I found joy was in watching Eddie and Joey form their brotherhood. Eddie looked at Joey like he was the earth, moon, and stars. I realized I had given birth to my best friends. I would do anything for them. I wanted to give them a better life than I could give them if I stayed in this marriage.

Rob and I divorced, and it got messy quickly. On the cusp of thirty, my life was coming apart. It was a horrible experience, but I knew I was doing the right thing for myself and my children, even though we lost everything, including the house and the car. Joey, Eddie, and I moved in with a mom friend of a friend who was also separated with kids. It was a weird setup, but it helped me get back on my feet. Then I met Eric, and a month into our whirlwind romance, I got pregnant—with twins.

I told Eric I wasn't expecting anything from him, given the circumstances. But he wanted to move in together right away. He bought a house and three months later, we had this big blended family: my two boys, who were five and seven at the time, fraternal boy twins on the way, and Eric's son from another relationship. We joked that we had become the Black Brady Bunch. Our instant family of five boys was beautiful, chaotic, and so much fun. But Eric and I were very different personalities. I loved him, but a familiar worry started to creep in: What if he was the wrong person?

When the twins were about three, I got an opportunity to work for Apple in Cupertino. I had left education and started in retail at Apple shortly after the twins were born and had worked my way up. At first, Eric encouraged me; he knew my dream was to advance to corporate. I was thrilled to get the job. But then, two days before we were due to move, Eric told me he wouldn't be joining us. He wanted to stay in Chicago's South Side near his family. I was devastated, but I had a stronger sense of myself by then and I knew what was important to me. I wouldn't let this sink me. I had a new life to lead and my own dreams to follow.

My parents and sisters were excited for me to move—and so were my sons. Joey, who was in fifth grade, noticed right away that California was more diverse and inclusive than his insular world in Chicago. We all became more proud, more comfortable in our identities in California. That sense of possibility, that everyone belonged, was amazing and freeing. After years of not being sure where I fit in, I realized that I got to define who I am, no one else. In January 2017, I did finally take my DNA tests. I wanted confirmation from my genetic makeup that my soul had not been steering me wrong. And it hasn't. I am a proud Afro-Indigenous woman with roots in Poland and Chile. But my journey with motherhood continued.

We'd been living in California for a few years when I met Mike on a night out with some friends. He watched me debate about policing and race—as the mother of Black sons, I have some thoughts—and with his eyes on me, I felt like the smartest person in the room. His smile lit me up. But after having fallen in love with the wrong person twice, I wanted to take it slow.

Once we started dating exclusively, it was clear he was the one I'd been waiting for. He's this amazing old-school provider and protector. He's the person who checks where the exits are, who keeps an emergency kit in his car. He's such a good dad.

Mike didn't have kids, and he made it clear that he was committed to me and my children. He didn't expect to have a baby with me. But all I could think was **How amazing would it be to have a baby with this guy? How can I give him that experience?** I felt like I'd won the lottery when I got pregnant at forty-two but then I miscarried after a few weeks. Nine months later, we found out I was pregnant again. It was a tough pregnancy with some bleeding, and COVID protocols made it complicated too. By twenty weeks, I finally accepted that I wasn't going to lose the pregnancy.

Our daughter, Kailani, was born on June 17, 2020. The boys, who are now twenty-one, nineteen, and fourteen, are thrilled to have a sister in our family. When my boys were babies, I couldn't wait until they were older. But with Kailani, I've found this amazing patience for the current moment. Physically, my back hurts all the time because I'm older, but on the flip side, I'm wiser and more mature now.

I haven't cut the straightest path to motherhood

or even to being myself, but I feel not only unapologetically okay with that, I'm proud of it. My children have a really special idea of family. They're absolutely devoted and protective of each other as siblings. I hope I've shown them how to love and count on each other. I know I've done my best to show them how to be proud of themselves and who they are.

And I hope they understand that life is a journey of growth. Recently, Joey said, "Mom, I didn't do as good as I wanted in my first semester at college but I'm learning." That's what we want for our kids: that they know that no matter who you are today, you can always be someone different. You can be someone better tomorrow. It's up to you. In the end, your identity belongs to you.

Recovery from Perfectionism

ADRIENNE BOSH

Philanthropist

Mothers have always been my heroes. I put them on a pedestal, starting with my grandmother, who was one of the most tough but graceful, family-driven women I've ever known. I've always been inspired by the idea of what a mother is: She's someone who makes your whole world better. She's always in your corner. There's no stopping a mom; her energy is infinite.

Here's the catch: As a mother myself, I know that none of this is true. That description of what a mom is and does is just **too** perfect, right? I think of my own mother, a single mom who had me while she was in college studying to be a nurse. She'd do double shifts at the hospital and come home exhausted. I saw how hard she worked just to hold it all together. Her energy was definitely **not** infinite, though I'm still in awe of how much she accomplished.

It wasn't until the birth of my twins that I understood for myself that mothers can't be heroes all the time. After my first two babies were born, I bounced back pretty quickly, but after the arrival of Lennox and Phoenix, I had to be brutally honest with myself: I was **not** okay. I didn't have **anything** together. It was a fall from grace, or so I thought. Looking at it now, I can see that it was a recovery from perfectionism. I had to learn how to give myself more love and patience, and by extension, to give the same to **all** mothers around me.

From the start, Chris and I were on the same page about children. Early in our relationship, when I was about twenty-four years old, I told him I wanted up to five kids. I was blown away when he said he wanted a big family too. Usually people talk about five kids like it would be a nightmare, so when he spoke about it enthusiastically, I fell all the more in love. Chris was already the sunshine in my world, but after that conversation, the sun shined that much brighter.

In August 2010, we got engaged. He already had a daughter, Trinity, from a prior relationship, so committing to him was, in a sense, signing on to be a bonus mother right away. She was part of the five-kids dream for us, so it was one down, four more to go! In July 2011, we married and started trying right away.

I found out I was pregnant via a blood test after the honeymoon. Besides some nausea, things were fairly easy for me, until around thirty-seven weeks, when the baby's movements slowed down. The doctor thought it was because the baby was getting bigger and didn't have as much room as before. I tried to trust the doctor, but my body just didn't feel right. I went home after that appointment and Chris, who was flying out that afternoon to New York for the playoffs, was like, "Are you good?" I said I was, but I sent him off, thinking, **What do I know?** I told myself that this must just be what pregnancy feels like toward the end.

That night, though, I was back in the hospital having contractions. They discovered that the cord was wrapped around the baby's neck, and recommended a C-section. Chris, who was now flying back from New York, was in the air, unreachable. The epidural I'd already received slowed down the contractions but didn't stop them. For a while, I was in a holding pattern—I really wanted to talk to Chris before making a decision—but then we couldn't wait any longer. Thankfully, just as they were prepping me for surgery, Chris finally arrived.

The C-section was miserable—I was throwing up the whole time—but Jackson came out fine. I was relieved that he was healthy, which is something you take for granted until you have a baby with health struggles. They put him on my chest and he made these little hungry sounds. I felt like we'd safely made it to the other side, and to share that moment with Chris, who almost didn't make it in time, was amazing.

My recovery was smooth; I was back at Chris's games in a couple of weeks. We had a night nurse, and my mom visited, but mostly we learned the ropes of being parents on our own. Right away, I mastered this magical dance for calming Jackson. It was a hop and sway kind of thing with a set beat. I could do it anywhere. Like, we'd be flying back from All-Stars with all these players around, and I'd stand up in the middle of the aisle and do my sway and hop. Traveling was, and still is, a big part of our life. We knew that we wanted our kids to experience everything with us, so if that meant having to pack a few extra suitcases of formula or diapers on a trip, then that's what we did.

The thing about wanting five kids is that by number two, you're still nowhere near the finish line. I got pregnant with number three before Jackson was two years old. Dylan came out via a planned C-section, healthy and strong.

Once again, I bounced back really quickly. In the hospital, I was changing my own clothes and leaning over to give her a bath with no problems. At home, having two babies to manage was a whole new game, but I still felt confident. Fortunately, Dylan was a baby who loved a consistent eating and sleeping schedule.

When I learned I was pregnant with twins, we were excited. A new challenge! From the outset, the pregnancy was incredibly different. I was "high-risk" just because it was twins, but then I was also diagnosed with low thyroid function and had to be put on medication. It was awesome to experience two babies growing inside of me, but it was also **very** physically uncomfortable. My stomach just took on a whole life of its own.

Around twenty-eight weeks, I went into labor, but the doctors were able to stop it. The next time, I was around thirty weeks and they gave me a shot to help develop the babies' lungs, along with medication to stop labor. They told me to go home and really take it easy because they wouldn't be able to stop labor again. Around thirty-three weeks, I finally went into full labor.

From the first moment on the operating table, everything seemed to go wrong. They numbed me, and maybe because I'm only five feet tall, the numbness climbed a bit higher than regular. I couldn't see or feel myself breathing. I actually asked Chris to tell me if I was still breathing, because I felt so scared and disconnected from my body.

They got one baby out, but he was whisked away immediately. Things got blurry then, but I know that shortly after that, they jabbed a shot in my arm and that jolted me back into consciousness. I was worried: The second baby was out now, but he wasn't placed on my chest either. I'd just had two babies and I didn't get to see or hold either one. One of them was put on a breathing machine right away, and then a few minutes later, both of them needed to go to the NICU for breathing and feeding tubes. Chris wanted to know whether he should stay with me, or go with the boys. I told him to go. I wanted all of our energy put toward the twins; I wasn't thinking at all about myself anymore.

Eventually, I got to put them on my chest in the NICU, but it was difficult because they were hooked up to so much machinery. Breathing machines, oxygen monitors, feeding tubes, all these cords everywhere. It was scary to hold them; I worried that I'd unhook something, that I'd break them.

For me, nothing was the same after that C-section. In the OR, it had taken forever to sew me up because my uterus wasn't going back to the right position. Afterward, in my hospital room, I wasn't able to dress myself or go to the bathroom or walk around. There was more blood than there had ever been before. I had a fever and felt extremely weak. What had happened to me? I kept telling everybody that something just didn't feel right. Eventually, we followed up with a scan of my uterus and that's when they said I had a "boggy" or "lazy" uterus, pick your term—either one feels like you're being shamed as a woman and mother.

They wanted me to stay at the hospital, but I would've been on a different floor from the NICU. I also had my other kids at home, wondering about me. So I got a PICC line surgically placed in my arm. I had to administer my own intravenous antibiotics and other medication every six hours for six weeks. Nothing in my body was behaving like it normally did. My uterus was not contracting, my stomach wasn't shrinking back to something like its usual appearance.

It was the most difficult time as a mom. I didn't feel like myself. I felt like a loser. I couldn't be there for my kids at home **or** at the hospital; I couldn't even get out of bed. Some days, I had to decide if I was going to take an hour to play with my kids or I was going to take a shower. I only had enough energy for one of those things. My iron was low; I was sick and running a fever. The twins came home a couple of weeks after birth, and I didn't feel close to ready for them.

I couldn't figure out where it all went wrong. Was I experiencing delayed bonding because I didn't get to hold them after their births? Or because they were in the NICU for so long? **Is something wrong with my mind?** I thought. **Why isn't this bad mood something I can just flip off, like a switch?** At the same time, there was so much to be grateful for: I had medical support for myself, NICU nurse support at home for the babies, and nanny support. But none of those things changed the fact that I was worried for my own survival and my babies' survival. As if that wasn't enough, my husband's issue with blood clots returned; this time the clot was in his leg, but the last one, in 2015, had traveled to his lungs and left him hospitalized.

It was the first time my husband didn't feel invincible to me, and it was the first time I had ever felt not invincible to myself. I think I was scared to even attach to the twins because I was afraid of losing them. I disconnected from everything. I tried going through the motions of being a mom, hoping it would all feel normal eventually, but nothing was clicking. Some of my friends, maybe because they were so used to me being active and always there for them, weren't as understanding as they could have been. My tribe wasn't the same one that's around me today.

Chris is my best friend, but trying to explain the size of the blood clot I had just passed was not what I wanted to talk about with him. I still wanted him to see me in a certain way. I prided myself on keeping that veil up. But then I'd ask myself: If you're not talking about it to him, then who? I had a doula friend who I talked to sometimes but it wasn't quite the same as having a doula who's been at your side the entire pregnancy. Looking back on my motherhood journey, I would definitely recommend or encourage an expecting mother to consider adding a doula or a midwife to be by her side.

Life was stressful for quite a while. I had double hernia surgery, another physical consequence from carrying twins. I stayed on thyroid medication and eventually was prescribed an antianxiety medication. For two years, with all that going on, I felt like a balloon on a string up in the sky, watching my own life below. Now I can talk about what happened, I can even unpack it, but it took a long time to get here. Medication helped, but I worked my way back to being fully present in my own life by granting myself grace and patience. I had to tell myself that I wasn't a failure as a mother. Part of me didn't want to complain, because it's not like anyone forced me to have all these kids. I didn't want to be ungrateful but at the same time, I had to accept that this was my story, that I was struggling but that was okay. Eventually, I would claw my way back to the light.

For the sake of all mothers, I want stories like mine to be normalized. I want people to know that even with support systems, or even if you've had other successful pregnancies and births, you might still struggle, and that is okay. It can come in so many forms: Systemic racism at the hospital might affect your treatment, or a lack of health insurance, or maybe you don't have a community to lean on. This lack of resources, especially for women of color, is part of what pushed me to start training as a doula. I now believe that doula work should be basic knowledge for all of us; I would love for it to be taught in high school!

People, especially now during the coronavirus pandemic, are starting to realize that mothers are not magicians. The meals that are prepared, the laundry that's folded, and the flowers that are placed on the nightstand, that's a mother's effort, that's not magic. I had to confront that reality myself: Motherhood isn't always easy and pretty. I don't say that to discourage anyone from having kids; my children are my whole world. But it's important to understand that motherhood is not about being perfect; it's about being fully present. Now that Lennox and Phoenix are four, I'm savoring each moment. They are the last of my babies and I'm not rushing through anything. Children aren't the only ones learning and growing all the time. I learned that, while community support is key, I also had to build a loving support system within myself. Otherwise, I can't be present to soak in the best moments. When I watch my children light up with the purest joy when they finally understand something new, it makes all my struggles feel worth it.

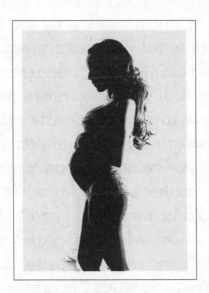

A Sacred Ritual
LATHAM THOMAS
Doula and Founder of Mama Glow

When it comes to how one becomes a mother, there's a difference between planning and preparation. In my work as a doula, families have shared their mindfully planned pregnancies—how they practiced meditation, or adjusted their lifestyle. Those are beautiful ways to come to pregnancy, but if you don't get to conscientiously plan your journey, that doesn't mean you're unprepared. Our life paths prepare us. I'm now not only the mother of a son, but I've become a guide for other mothers and birthing people before, during, and after birth, as well as through loss. My decades of experience have taught me that there are many paths to preparation.

I was twenty-three when I became pregnant with Fulano, who is now an adult. I was a recent Columbia

University grad still living in New York City. In many ways, I still needed my own parents. But I was guided through the journey by ancestral wisdom and an internal knowing that was nurtured during my childhood.

When I was four, my mother became pregnant with my younger sister. This experience of watching her body support a life planted the first seed in the lush garden of my own motherhood journey. As a four-year-old, I was the perfect height to track my mother's growing belly. My aunt and my great-aunt were pregnant too and all due within a month of each other. These radiant Black women would talk freely about their changing bodies and my mom always welcomed me into conversations. She taught me the principles of sacred anatomy and I learned how to name and talk about my body parts. She made sure I had access to books and PBS programs that helped shape my understanding of the body. This instilled a sense of empowerment and autonomy that would inform my entire life and reproductive journey. One time in the grocery store, a woman commented, "Wow, your mom has a baby in her belly." And I swiftly corrected her. "No, my mommy has a baby in her uterus and it's going to come out of her vagina."

While my mother raised me, and eventually my younger sister, as a single mother in Oakland, my father, a pilot living in Southern California, visited often. They were great co-parents. I was raised with a village; my grandparents, aunts, and uncles were also pivotal in our upbringing. My sister and I saw my grandmother every day after school. Granny always had freshly baked homemade pound cake waiting on a cake stand for us. Traditionally, Black families are matrilineal, multigenerational, and inclusive. We are not bound by the nuclear family standard; instead, we embrace village keeping, which includes caregiving from relatives and family friends. There were some people who were around so much in my childhood that I was shocked when I eventually learned they weren't blood kin.

When I became a mother, I knew that I wanted that same sense of community for my child. The night that my partner, Nemo, and I conceived, I recognized at the very moment that something sacred took place. Soon after, I felt the weight and shape of my breasts change, a constant feeling of fullness, yet I was still surprised when I got a positive blood test a month later. When I told Fulano's father, he was ready and excited to embrace the new reality. Not long before, he'd taken a silent retreat in Budapest and had emerged from that experience knowing he wanted a family.

Still, outside of his support, I didn't have a local village to lean on. In 2003, social media was barely in existence so I had to build my own community of new parents and parents-to-be. I met some people through birthing classes, which I saw as a continuation of my college education in the life sciences.

After I emerged from first trimester fatigue, we were thrilled to discover that New York City had just outlawed smoking in clubs so we went dancing! Pretty soon, I was inviting other pregnant women I knew from classes to come out with us, and meeting other pregnant women who went to clubs too. As my village grew, I felt more anchored in my journey to becoming a mother.

Next to one of our favorite nightclubs was the Elizabeth Seton Childbearing Center, the first free-standing birth center in the nation. Nemo suggested we try it out, but I figured that they wouldn't take my insurance. But it ended up being a haven for me. Not only did they have super-low co-pays, they always gave you access to your chart. You were responsible for taking your weight, testing your urine, and writing down your results on your chart. And they photocopied your entire file for you. I still have all the notes every midwife wrote after seeing me. Having that kind of control over my clinical care was incredibly empowering to me. I always felt supported and listened to by the midwives, never dismissed, ignored, or micro-aggressed. The medical-industrial complex is rooted in racism and has a deep history with harm toward Black women and seeing us as strong and impervious to pain. A 2019 study published in the **American Journal of Emergency Medicine** analyzed data from fourteen previously published studies on pain management and found that Black patients were 40 percent less likely to receive medication for acute pain compared to white patients. A 2016 study found that nearly half of first- and second-year medical students believed that Black people have "thicker skin" than white people, and that we experience less pain than white people. While in bondage our ancestors endured non-consensual medical experimentation with no anesthesia, for the advancement of medicine. This is the unatoned-for legacy of a system that serves us today. That location of Elizabeth Seton closed a few months after my son's birth, due to the skyrocketing costs of malpractice insurance, and I was crushed because we all need access to the midwifery model of care.

At nearly forty-one weeks pregnant, I was told by the midwives that if I went beyond forty-two weeks, I'd have to be induced at a hospital because my chances of stillbirth increased. I didn't want anything to do with the hospital—that wasn't part of my vision. That weekend, Nemo and I walked miles traversing the city in the sweltering July heat. On this particular evening, the moon's face was fully illuminated. It was a Buck Moon, the Native American name for July's full moon. Male deer shed their antlers every year and begin to regrow them in July, hence the name. As I was getting ready for bed around midnight, I pleaded for a sign from the baby that labor was coming. I asked God to shed my ego, fortify and prepare me. Nemo was playing this Mahalia Jackson record and she was "scraping the pan," aka, hitting a soulful growl. Seconds after the crescendo, I felt this pop and then warmth. My water had broken. I stood up and it was like a full bucket had splashed onto the hardwood floor. I was mopping it up when my son's godfather-to-be, Kiernan, walked in. I told him, "Wait, wait, the mucus plug is out here somewhere, you gotta back up." A big blob of mucus isn't the kind of thing you want to leave on the floor. We found it, and then we waited for labor to truly kick in. The midwives told me to go to bed but instead, I watched jazz documentaries with Kiernan till 6 A.M., too excited to shut my eyes. By 8 A.M., the contractions had gotten intense. I showered and tried to sleep, but the labor was too strong for me to rest. Between moans, I told Nemo that it was time to go to the birth center.

Nemo called his father to come over. At the door, Papa Rick was a wreck, screaming about how we needed to hurry. Nemo tried to calm him down, but it didn't really take. We all packed into a cab—Nemo, me, Kiernan, and Nemo's father—to take us the seven blocks to the birth center with Papa Rick yelling at the driver, "Step on it, we gotta get **moving**!"

At Elizabeth Seton, three birth attendants waited for me in reception, a nurse midwife, midwife, and a midwife in training. Nemo's dad barked that I needed a bedroom but they ignored him. Instead, they focused on me. Completely silent, they watched as I cycled through a few contractions, tracking me in the process. Then they guided me to a birth suite. Their silent, expert focus shifted the tone entirely. The moment was not about rushing or intensity; it was about surrendering to this primal work.

In a dark room with just Nemo, I labored in a tub with jets. I drifted in and out for a few hours, having these crazy dreams. I tried to tell Nemo about them, but then the next contraction blotted out everything. My son's godmother-to-be arrived. The midwives didn't hover, they just checked in now and again, listening to the baby's heartbeat. When it was clear that our son was coming soon, the midwives had me get out of the tub. Later, Nemo told me that they had exchanged a look, like something was wrong.

The nurses heard my son's heartbeat slowing down as he was descending through the vaginal passageway. In that situation, it was safer to have the baby out of the tub, so they helped me onto the queen-sized bed. I crawled on the soft quilt and squatted, with Nemo supporting my arm on one side, and my son's godmother-to-be on the other.

Then something extraordinary happened, a moment of ancestral calling that would transform my life in many ways: I felt this heat above me, and I looked up to see a horseshoe-shaped formation. My ancestors were there shoulder to shoulder gazing down on me. I didn't recognize their faces, but there was a soul recognition. I pointed up to what looked like the plain old ceiling to everyone else and said, "I want to go there." Then I left my physical body and hovered over myself, watching my son being born. My astral body could see everything, things my earthly body could not have seen, like my son crowning. When Fulano was born, I felt an overflow of joy. It was endorphins, oxytocin, DMT, but also this spiritual knowledge that I had been ushered across the threshold into motherhood by my ancestors. They ensured a safe crossing for Fulano and me, and they were also calling me to become a guide for safe passage for others too.

After Fulano was born, the room was so peacefully quiet. He curled up next to me as I rode this blissful high. When I could finally talk again, I said, "I have to protect this experience for women." Birth should be an opportunity to revel in one's divinity, to experience transcendence, to embody a holy ritual. Though it would take me a while to process, and heed, the part of my ancestors' message that called me to be a guide for others, I knew I had received the exact birth I needed to catapult me into my life's work.

Only a few hours later, I was traveling the seven blocks home with Nemo and our newborn baby. Fulano was covered up in a borrowed car seat as we walked through Manhattan on a seemingly regular Sunday afternoon. But I was transformed. There were double rainbows in the sky after an earlier rain, and the Buck Moon the night before. I was happy that Fulano had chosen such an auspicious day to be born.

My mother came out the next day to stay with us. She's a great project manager type so she made sure guests didn't stay too long and that I was sleeping and eating well. My mother has a gift with breastfeeding—as a baby, I breastfed exclusively until I was one—so she made me hot compresses and helped with latching. I ended up nursing Fulano till he was three and it was a grounding experience for both of us.

Fulano loved being physically close to me and Nemo, and we loved providing that warmth. For a long time, he slept in the bed with us. Random people in our lives tried to discourage us from this practice, but in the end, it didn't matter what anyone else thought, because a family bed worked for us. As a doula, I can't emphasize enough to new parents that it's not about following the advice you'll get from your mother, or experts, or the stranger on the street. What worked for one child may not work for another. Instead, I help parents unlock their own intuition so they can make the decisions aligned with their needs.

After I had time to process its meaning, I followed through on the message I was given in the birthing suite. In 2011, I founded Mama Glow, a global maternal health company that centers on reproductive justice and birth equity. We educate and empower culturally competent and trauma-informed doulas around the world to meet the needs of the modern parent, especially in this current landscape of crisis. In this country, the maternal death rate is disproportionately high for Black women, Latinas, and Native American women in comparison to white women. Black women in particular are **four times** more likely to die during childbirth or due to childbirth-related causes than white women. This is unacceptable! In the postpartum period, one in four women return to work only ten days after having a baby. That's not enough time to heal physically or to bond with our newborns. Doulas provide critical support along the perinatal continuum where we are met with policy gaps.

Black communities are often matrilineally driven, so when a mother dies, it disorganizes our community. Not just the community of her immediate family, but her relatives, her friends, her neighbors— that loss knows no boundaries. Every time a mother has a childbirth-related death and isn't able to raise her children, it injures our cultural ecosystem.

In the moment that I joined with my ancestors during Fulano's birth, I didn't know I would become initiated into birth work, which is an ancient practice that runs deep in our legacy. When I teach, I feel the presence of my grandmother and other foremothers in our lineage. Everyone who answers the call to doula work is serving a legacy so much bigger than a single one of us.

If loss and trauma can touch an untold number of souls and circumstances, so can resilience and empowerment. If a person is empowered through birth, then they can become empowered in other ways: They also feel empowered to ask for a raise, or to ask for what they like in the bedroom, or to march to protest police violence. If a birthing person is witnessed in their vulnerability, and also given permission to show their strength at the same time, well, when a person comes out the other side of that experience, nobody can tell her shit. When I think about who I was before I gave birth to Fulano, who's now attending the Berklee College of Music, I was just a girl. After Fulano, I am completely another person. From the moment of my son's birth, with my ancestors guiding me, I was reborn and became a new version of myself.

My Favorite Story

RACHEL FEINSTEIN

Comic

SEPTEMBER 2019

I hate parks. I feel sorry for women pushing swings. I assume anyone who's pushing a swing needs to be rescued. It looks like such sad, monotonous activity. I always figure the women who happily push swings make the best moms, though. And I never relate to them. They're seasonal decorators with Easter place mats who intrinsically know when pasta is done. They call themselves "Mama Bear" on Instagram. Their IG profile headings say things like "Boxed wine is my juice box!"

I'm teeming with ADD. I lose a debit card every week. There is peanut butter with a key stuck in it in my purse right now. And I'm a comic. Also, I'm sort of a sarcastic asshole.

How can I have a kid?

But I do love children. I used to be a nanny. It was the only job I didn't get fired from besides stand-up, even though I was constantly losing the kids' shoes and the parents' keys. I always figured I'd have one of my own one day, but I've been so focused on my career that I've kept kicking the ball down the road. Now, after a year of marriage, I decide I should get my eggs checked to see if they're rancid or not.

This pushy Upper West Side lady at SoulCycle recommends a fertility doctor. She's one of those women who act like you only have one choice when you're making a decision. I love people like this because I hate choices.

"You **must** go to **this** daycare."

"You **must** see **this** doctor."

"You **have** to get **this** shampoo or all your hair will fall out."

Thank you, Sharon Weismann, this is exactly the kind of advice I need. My life is derailed by too many choices. That's half the reason I stop everything I start. It's the reason I may not finish this essay!

The SoulCycle–endorsed doctor says my egg situation looks pretty bleak. Something is wrong with my hormones. He thinks this could be caused by a possible benign brain tumor that's causing them to read at pre-menopausal levels. Suddenly, I'm devastated. I didn't even want to be pregnant.

I'd rather pay a broad in Pennsylvania to have a kid for me if I could come up with cash. I just want that **choice**, and, of course, to not be menopausal.

So, while I wait on my tumor results and get used to my new menopausal identity, I focus on work.

Fine, good. This is fate. I'm not supposed to have a kid. I once drank candle wax because I thought it was mulled wine. I'm the woman that mothers go see with their "hubbies" on date nights and on the way home the man hugs his wife a little tighter because he realizes how classy she is in comparison to that fun-loving dirty girl they just watched onstage. He thinks, **That broad was fun for a raunchy evening, but look at what a lady I have. I don't rub her knee enough.**

OCTOBER 2019

I'm feeling pretty good. I sell a pilot idea about my life as a comic married to an FDNY captain. It's the biggest thing to happen in my career so far.

I feel less weird about my possible tumor and all the blood tests. My husband Pete doesn't seem to be turned off by my new collection of menopausal capes. I even start feeling okay about possibly not being able to have a family. It's hard enough to be the only loud Jewish stand-up in the world of FDNY Staten Island dinner dances, I don't need to be the outsider in the mom-world too. And I'll never have to push a swing!

But then I start to feel nauseous, and everything smells like piss and rotting takeout.

I don't take a pregnancy test because we had a miscarriage before and I don't want to get Pete's hopes up and then down again. So, we go back to SoulCycle doctor. And I'm pregnant.

"But wait, I thought I had mangled 'mones and a brain tumor! I've been drinking without a care in the world." The doc just breezes past that. "Nope, none of that, there's the heartbeat. There's your baby."

Pete is so happy. I'm scared shitless.

The pilot is supposed to shoot in March, and it doesn't involve a pregnancy. I start covering my bump with a lot of oversized Paula Poundstone blazers and obsessing over how to tell the network. I'm depressed. I don't want to make the choice between pilot and kid. There's no one bad man explicitly telling me I have to, but there's just no room for both to exist. There's no maternity leave in stand-up, this isn't the story I sold them, and it's supposed to shoot in March, when I'll be a heinous whale.

Or maybe I'm just terrified to have a miscarriage again. To have my body let everyone down again.

NOVEMBER 2019

It's a Friday night in November and I'm headlining at Gotham Comedy Club. It's a sold-out show and I'm killing. No one seems distracted by the fact that I'm dressed like Bea Arthur in my cover-up pregnancy smock. I have at least forty more minutes left of my set when I feel blood running down my leg.

Am I having a miscarriage?

Part of me is terrified, distracted, running through potentially catastrophic scenarios and wondering if the audience can see me bleeding. But another part is having **the best** time I've had onstage in months.

Anyone who does stand-up knows you have to think about so many different things onstage:

Is that red-faced drunk about to heckle me or is he just so drunk or is he just muttering to himself?

Is that the light that tells me I have to wrap up or is it just someone's iPhone?

Am I having a miscarriage?

Can that couple see the miscarriage on my leg?

Somehow, there I am, half-panicked with my legs slammed together, having the time of my life. Comics are adrenaline junkies. The highs are so high and the lows are so low. It's a bipolar career. You can do a set on Conan one night and then the next night you're in Toledo and someone throws a soft taco at your tit, my tit. You can also have the best set, with every single person laughing except one dude who's just not buying it, sitting there with his arms folded. I'll never forget what my friend and late comic Mike DeStefano told me when we were on **Last Comic Standing** together and I asked him, "How come I choose to focus on that one disgusted expression in a crowd of laughter?"

"Because that's the one you believe."

That night in November, I even get the folded-arms guy to unfold them.

Offstage, I take pictures with drunk girls who have no idea I was about to run to the bathroom and check for a miscarriage.

There is a lot of blood.

I Uber to the closest emergency room. Pete is out on an emergency run and I can't reach him.

I love being married to a firefighter. I tell servers at restaurants, "I'll have a ginger ale. He's a fireman." I wear his captain's hat around the apartment and make him take his badge out at CVS when he's buying gum.

It's all fun and games except for moments like this.

This is the first time he is essential to me and to someone else.

They hook me up to an IV and give me a sonogram. The technician says nothing at all to me, just stares at his computer and robotically types as I wait to see if my baby is alive. The medical equivalent to the folded-arms guy. Finally, I prop myself up.

On the screen, all I can see are the words "Feinstein, Vag Bleed."

Is that all I am, I think. Feinstein Vag Bleed? Is this what it's all going to boil down to?

The doctor comes in and says the amount of blood leads him to believe that the baby won't make it. The hemorrhage is just too big. He tells me to follow up with my ob-gyn. I'll probably have a miscarriage and then need this operation called a DNC, which is what you do when you have an "unviable" baby in you. I keep calling it "Democratic National Committee" to distract him—and myself—from my own lonely, tragic moment.

Now, I really, really want this baby to make it, and I feel wildly guilty for ever feeling conflicted.

It's the loneliest cab ride home. The next day, Pete comes home from the firehouse with a "Sorry You're Hemorrhaging" donut and a "Sorry You're Miscarrying" card. I'm ashamed that my body is letting us down and I **really** don't want to see him cry in his hands in the ob-gyn's office.

We go to the doctor and she says, "Nope, baby is healthy. That was a subchorionic hemorrhage but it corrected itself." Not sure how anything inside my body had the ability to self-correct, so I'll just give credit to the healing power of drunken late-show approval.

FEBRUARY 2020

My hypochondriac friends are rambling about the coronavirus. The same ones that warned me about bird flu are telling me I have to buy weird amounts of toilet paper and soup. I mock them. I don't really believe in germs. I worry more about people being mad at me than I worry about dying.

MARCH 2020

March is when it gets weird, though. Tom Hanks gets it and a couple guys from the Golden State Warriors and suddenly we're like, **Oh maybe we all can get it too. Since we have so much in common . . .**

I'm in Florida for a gig. My shows are full because it's business as usual there even though there's not a roll of toilet paper left in Brooklyn and people are running with loaves of bread in the streets. I feel guilty for performing, but I need the money for the baby. My worst fears when I got pregnant were that I'd be isolated and dependent.

All I think about the first night onstage is whether I'm killing the baby, so I decide to cancel the rest of my shows. Everyone at home is mad that I'm in Florida and everyone in Florida is mad that I'm canceling. Suddenly, my fears are coming true but for completely different reasons. I'm totally dependent on my husband, and terrified that he's going to come home from the firehouse soaked with COVID. I can't work. I'm locked in my apartment. And the germ people were right! We are living in one of those pandemic movies that I hate. At least if we're going to be living in a surreal movie, couldn't it be a genre I like? Like, true crime?

At first, the hardest part about quarantining while pregnant isn't missing my loved ones, blowouts, and spray tans. It's not doing stand-up.

Whatever god-awful nonsense life hurls at me, I can always get up onstage and creatively bitch about it. It's great because you don't need to rely on four other dudes and equipment to perform. It's just you and whatever you want to say. You tweak to fit a million factors: how drunk, how PC, how smart, how dumb, how young, how old. But it's still all you and your own stories. It's your little closing arguments to the world.

Stand-up is a little bin where I put all my complaints. I need my bin! For all those weird, accidentally funny, relatable parts of life, the snarled moments that don't fit. But comics are un-essential workers. We're the very last on the list: phase twenty of reopening.

APRIL 2020

The sirens blare all day and night. It's weird and lonely. The rich people have fled to their summer homes. When things like this happen, it really makes you realize who has summer homes. Pete hurts his shoulder in a fire, so he's put on light duty and I am insanely grateful. I want to keep punching him in the arm.

He's a researcher. He attacks having a kid in a pandemic anxiety by watching endless YouTube tutorials about diaper hacks. Every night he falls asleep in his uniform watching **Mom and Baby Jackson's Tummy Time Tips**. All I want to do is watch **Forensic Files**.

One day, I realize that no one has seen me looking pregnant. I'd been focusing so much on trying to hide it, dressing like a district attorney. Suddenly, that feels sort of sad. So instead of a shower, I put on a motherly floral sundress and take a gentle walk around the block, cupping my bump. Hipsters look at me with sad eyes over their Etsy face masks. One lady actually clutches her husband's arm and says, "Could you imagine?"

I like their sympathy. It feels like all I have. I can't go onstage and get that validation anymore. And **yeah, this does suck!**

We find out I have gestational diabetes, which makes it a high-risk pregnancy. I have virtual diabetic appointments because our hospital is having a corona outbreak. People give lots of advice:

"You **must** have a home birth. Hospitals are too dangerous right now."

"You **need** to quarantine from your husband!"

No home birth. And I'm not strong enough to do this without him. Instead, I decide to make a diabetic cake. I go out and buy the ingredients at an actual store, wearing latex gloves and a mask, and the whole endeavor feels somehow like a triumphant, defiant act. And that's when I realize I've fallen into a low-grade depression.

Officials say women in New York City have to give birth alone. No partner in the room. I can do my sympathy strolls and bang on a pan to support the actual heroes. I can prick my finger five times a day and write down what I eat and then lose the pad on which I wrote it. But I cannot give birth alone. We manage to switch to a hospital upstate.

MAY 20, 2020

I hear the doctors whisper to each other during my C-section.

"She wants a tiny scar!"

"I know, she only told me that a hundred times."

My mother-in-law had told me, "The Brennan head will shred you. I was icing my vagina for weeks." So, I'd scheduled the C-section.

Her birth is fast. They've put me in this cold, bizarre room on a metal table. A labor nurse softly whispers helpful sentences to me and squeezes my hands while I get the epidural.

Then Pete comes in dressed like a robber and adjusts my face mask. And I feel that weird tug everyone warns you about—a heinous feeling. I say, "I think they're starting the surgery now." I figure I'll be lying there for another forty-five minutes. But after five minutes, they pull her right out and up! We did it!

She's swollen and has a hilarious frantic expression, probably how I would look if someone pulled me out of a stomach and into the dumb, combusting world.

Then, because of COVID, we aren't allowed to go outside at all, another choice made for us! So, we sit at home and stare at her and it is oddly **perfect.** I don't want any more choices other than this one. I like the choice the virus left us with.

We aren't allowed to have any visitors, and this becomes an odd blessing. There are a lot of benefits to a COVID birth, it turns out. No fear of missing out. No unwanted guests. All I have to say is, "Sorry, we're trying not to kill her."

I never read any book or article about giving birth before I did it. I was so busy reacting to the news and changing restrictions that I only bothered learning about what I couldn't do when pregnant (like use Retin-A, drink a 40, or see anyone). Now I think I focused so much on my fears and all the ways I'd be insufficient as a mother that I never considered the fun parts. How purely **entertaining** it is.

Surprisingly, becoming a mother didn't change me. I'm still a sarcastic asshole. I'm not going to call myself "Mama Bear" or buy magnets with bad wine jokes. I didn't suddenly develop the sense of humor of a weather girl from Toledo. I still hate parks! I just love being in them with her.

I still like all the same things too. Listening to stories, comics that tell stories. And she's my favorite story already. Any fact that is part of her story is immediately compelling to me.

I love every detail. Like, she has these absurdly long, interesting hands like a piano player and she curls them in the weirdest way like some sort of hand yoga. I take a video of these hand dances and

I lie in bed and watch it while she sleeps in the next room. To me, it's the very best movie. Better than a pandemic film. Better than a true-crime doc.

JUNE 10, 2020

Today I walk into the nursery and pick up the baby.

I have a lot of fear. I keep thinking about all these questions that I don't have any answer for. Will Pete be okay when he goes back to work? When will stand-up come back? When will I be slammed in a booth with my friends at the Comedy Cellar complaining about a drunk in the crowd? This seems like such a luxury now and maybe it always was.

I sit down on the perfectly made bed. It's only perfect because I have a baby nurse who's about to leave. I feel intensely grateful for her. She's teaching me everything I should have read in those books, and I really don't know how I'll cope without her. What if I leave my ADD meds on the floor and the baby eats them? The nurse knows everything, how to swaddle her and cut her tiny nails so she can do her hand dances without scratching her eyes. She knows how to fold a fitted sheet and arrange throw pillows. She definitely knows when pasta is done.

I'm staring at my daughter and trying hard not to think about any of these many things, trying to just focus on the moment and what a privilege it is to hold my healthy daughter and stare at her interesting hands.

Then suddenly, the nurse grabs my arm.

"Oh my god, you're bleeding all over the bed, are you okay?!"

I look down and I quickly realize it's not blood. Somehow, I've smeared fudge from the protein bar I was eating **all** over her bedspread. I've soiled the bed made perfectly by this lovely woman who's helping me care for my new baby during a global pandemic. I'm already a failure at this.

I look down and suddenly my baby starts crying with that panicked, piercing immediacy that only newborns can muster.

But it has nothing to do with the protein bar or the fudge, of course, or COVID or the blood that was never there. She doesn't care.

None of those story lines go anywhere. She just wants me, her mom.

Finally Filled In

ASHLEY GRAHAM

Supermodel and Entrepreneur

When I was seventeen, my parents gave me an ultimatum: You can move to New York and dive into modeling full-time, but if you don't make it within a year (as in, you need to support yourself), you have to move back to Nebraska and go to college. The prospect of college was daunting to me; I have ADD and dyslexia. And there was **nothing** I wanted more than to live in New York City and make it as a model. So, sure enough, within that first year, I did.

My parents grew up working hard: my mom on a farm, and my dad in a little Mississippi fishing town. Their ultimatum made me learn how to really hustle. I've always had a good work ethic, which served me well for a home birth.

As an older teen in New York, I was free and wild. I was figuring myself out and becoming who I was meant to be. I wasn't thinking about kids at all during this time! I knew I wanted children because my mom has always been my best friend, and I wanted a relationship like that with my own kids. But I didn't want to have them right away, like she had. If you ask her, she'll say she loved being a young mom. She'll say, about my two younger sisters and me, "But you girls were so much fun!" She always tells me that she doesn't regret staying at home with us, but I've always wanted to be established and be focused on my career. I wanted to know who I was first, I wanted time to make mistakes and learn from them.

Before Justin and I tied the knot in 2010—I was only twenty-two but we were ready—we discussed the question of children. We always said we wanted kids, but for a long time after we got married, our timing wasn't in sync. He'd want kids one day, and then I wouldn't. Then I would, and he wouldn't. Part of the problem was that we loved our transient lifestyle. Justin's a cinematographer and director so he's in Los Angeles a lot. And I'm always wherever my work is: Paris, Miami . . . all over the place. We'd go to Puerto Rico on a moment's notice, just because we could.

Finally, after nearly a decade of marriage, we decided to make the leap. By Nebraska standards, at age thirty-one, I should have already had one or two kids. I got off birth control for the first time in a decade and figured it would take a while. That was in January 2019; by Easter, I was pregnant.

We were thrilled but, still, we shed a few tears; our fast-track life was never going to be the same. My selfishness, gone! My husband and I had always been very independent, often living in different cities for work, but now we had to figure out how to share our lives more deeply. And what about this little person who would need me twenty-four/seven? Justin and I had some hard conversations about how we were going to make it work, logistically and emotionally, but ultimately, I felt rooted by our relationship. We love each other and know each other so well, and more important, we **like** each other. It might sound basic but to be able to parent with someone you genuinely like spending time with is so important.

In my first trimester, I always felt queasy, though I never threw up. An alien was taking over my body. I was supposed to go to The Ashram in California, where you're hiking, doing yoga, and eating vegan, but I had to cancel the week before. I could barely walk up a flight of stairs. I was so bummed about canceling, like, **Dang, this kid's already changing my plans.**

In my second trimester, I cried a lot. My husband had to pick me up after **many** breakdowns. My whole career, I've had control over my body. Whenever anyone tried to wrench that control away from me, I shut them down. I've molded and expanded the concept of beauty in this industry by taking ownership of my body, how it looks and is represented. But now, with this little baby growing inside of me, I was like, "Oh my god, I'm getting bigger and there's nothing I can do about it." I had to really talk to myself about what was going on. "Look," I'd say, "this weight is for the baby. Your body is beautiful and it's helping this baby to grow."

It was one thing to see my body changing so rapidly, but I was also confused by my harsh reaction to it. I've made a career out of telling women to be proud of their bodies, no matter what the scale or the beauty industry says. I had to go back and listen to my own messaging. When I was seventeen, I would use these affirmations: "I am bold. I am brilliant. I am beautiful." This time, I thanked each body part for its service: "Back, you are big and sturdy for this baby. Belly, you're growing big because there's a baby inside."

No one says this, ever, but my third trimester was a dream. I had so much energy. I found this amazing acupuncturist who helped me stay limber. I was able to work out four days a week, and I moved apartments. Finally, I was at peace with my body. Suddenly I was like, "Ooh, I'm naked. Someone take my picture!"

I can't say I've shaken every last bit of judgment from my brain. I gained fifty-five pounds and anytime a friend said, "Oh, I only gained thirty," I just couldn't wrap my mind around that. Like, **HOW did you only gain thirty pounds?** But I always had to remind myself: Every body is different. Every pregnancy is different. Every baby is different.

For my birth plan, I had no idea that there were more options beyond epidural or no epidural. My doula, the amazing Latham Thomas, asked me what kind of birth I wanted and I said, "I don't want an epidural because my mom didn't do an epidural. I want to be badass like her." Latham was like, "OK, cool." She was never biased towards anything; she just listened. As I got further along, she sent me some information about other options, along with ways to healthfully support my baby through good food and exercise, but she was always supportive of whatever I wanted to do.

At thirty-two weeks, I had a really negative experience with my OB, a very prominent doctor who had been recommended by a friend. While measuring my stomach, he asked if I wanted a planned C-section. I said, "No, I want to have a vaginal delivery." He was like, "Well, it's been scientifically proven that if you're on your back with your legs up, your baby will slide out better." I didn't say anything but I was arguing in my head, thinking, **What are you talking about? Scientifically proven? How?** Then he goes on: "Look, you're going to be in a lot of pain. You really should be open to Pitocin and an epidural. I think you should come in at thirty-nine weeks to get induced." I really didn't like the fact that he was already trying to talk me out of the experience I wanted, and I still had many weeks to go.

Around the same time, I found out that he was one of the top C-section doctors in New York. I started to read more about other birthing options. A big eye-opener was the 2008 documentary **The Business of Being Born,** which critiques the profit-minded way the American healthcare system approaches childbirth. It involves executive producer Ricki Lake's very positive experience with home birth but I was still intimidated by the idea. I thought a birth center could be a good middle ground but the closest one was forty-five minutes away. As I approached thirty-three weeks, I was praying so hard for the right option to make itself clear. I started interviewing midwives.

I knew after the first meeting with Kimm Sun and Kateryn Nunez of Heart Science Midwifery that I wanted them to deliver my baby. They have high standards for who gets to have a home birth. Are mom and baby healthy? Does Mom have an optimistic outlook on life? So much of being a mom is a mental game. You need to come into home birth as strong as you can be, on every level. I created a home gym and Justin and I would prac-tice birthing positions. I felt so relieved knowing I wouldn't have to go anywhere, and I thanked God that my baby and I were healthy enough to take this path.

At a very ripe forty-one weeks, Justin and I booked one last escape. That Tuesday, we rented out a beautiful Japanese spa called Shou Sugi Ban House on Long Island, all to ourselves. I'm so glad we got those last few precious moments together because by Friday, back in the city, Kateryn's sweep of my membranes kicked off these dull, achy cramps, like I was about to get my period.

I was craving beer and raw fish (it was very specific, nothing else would do). With the midwives' approval, we went to Nobu for the classiest fish and beer I could find. Later that night, we meditated together. By 5 A.M., I was howling like a wolf from full-on contractions. I didn't know that sound could come out of me! By 7 A.M., I told Justin we needed to get the house ready. The contractions had gotten milder and suddenly I was Mary Poppins wanting to scrub the floors.

I wasn't convinced yet that I was in real labor so we decided to carry on with our day. Our plan was to have the videographer come over for interviews about the birth because we love to document everything. Then brunch, yoga, and somehow I'd squeeze in a pedicure. The contractions kicked in again at brunch, though, and Justin was bright-eyed and bushy-tailed. He was like, "This is happening!" But I was like, "I'm not in labor. I'm not in labor." During yoga, I did a couple of Cat-Cows and boom: My water broke. I burst into tears, then hysterical crying. It was just so emotional because I knew what was coming.

Luckily, yoga was in my apartment building. As Justin helped me up the stairs, I started to black out a little. The back pain was excruciating. I stepped into the shower but soon enough I was in bed, crying out. Justin called Latham, Kimm, and Kateryn. When they arrived, I was on the birth ball, and so relieved to see them. I took it as a sign that maybe this would all be over soon. Ha! They checked my vitals and baby's heartbeat. Everything looked good but I was in such indescribable pain. It was a shock to my system. I thought I was a tough cookie but my god, I had no idea.

I went through six hours of labor after my water broke, sustained by all that cardio I'd done in my home gym. I cycled through probably eight different positions all around my apartment, and even in our pool. To get the baby into the birth canal, I lay in Justin's arms in a backbend while one of the midwives had a scarf around my hips that she pulled forward. I pushed on every contraction till the baby entered the canal.

Then we got into the pool, where I pushed for just under an hour. Girl, that ring of fire. Wow. I screamed, "Ring of Fire!!" Then, "Progress?" They answered, "We can feel the head!" I reached down and touched his soggy hair. It empowered me to keep going. He was so close.

Right when his head was about to come out, Kimm screamed at me to stand up. I stood up and I faced her. Quietly, she said, "Don't push for now. On the next contraction, push." I waited, then whoosh: Isaac was out with the umbilical cord wrapped once around his neck, but it was easily removed. I lay back and she plopped him on my chest. He was so teeny-tiny and sweet. He wasn't screaming, he was just like, **Hey.** His eyes were wide open. I said, "Nice to meet you." Justin and I had tears in our eyes. In that moment, I was meeting Isaac for the first time, but I already knew him. It was a little like online dating, how you can get to know a person online but when you meet them in person, it's a whole other feeling. All that you've imagined is finally filled in.

There was blood and vernix—the white protective coating that babies have on their skin in the womb—in the water, all over the pool. We kept his umbilical cord connected for about an hour, to get as much oxygen and blood out of the placenta as possible. I cried and thanked everybody. They helped me out of the pool, and it was five steps to my own bed, thank God. I thought I'd be able to just pop right up but no, **that vagina just went through full-on trauma, girlfriend. You're basically a war veteran now.**

I already knew what kind of mother I wanted to be. I wanted to be as chill as possible. Justin says I'm a lot softer as a person now. I'm not as quick with the tongue, I guess. Lots of people told me to get a night nurse, but I fed him myself through the night like my mom did for us. I try not to hover: I let Isaac explore while making sure everything is baby-proofed because, duh.

Basically, I try not to overthink it. This is my life and my kid. We decided early on that he's going to live our life, not the other way around. So far, Isaac has been very accommodating, but we'll see what happens later.

I Prayed Anyway

JILL SCOTT

Grammy Award–winning Singer/Songwriter, Actress, New York Times Bestselling Poet

Because of my Mother, GRANDMother, and Aunts, I've always been a big believer in speaking things into action. I'd seen them do it a thousand times.

When I was about fourteen, I wanted to stop my period. My menstrual cycle was debilitatingly painful. I could barely function for days on end. So I made a request. I asked God to take my cycle away, and bring it back when SHE was ready for me to have a baby. As unbelievable as it sounds, my cycle decreased; it came every three months, then once a year, and finally, not at all. I was happy and grateful (yay). I didn't think much about it until I was nineteen and in college. I went to Planned Parenthood to get checked out.

The doctor told me that all those years without my cycle hadn't been a blessing. I'd never have children. Never!?!? They recommended a hysterectomy. Said they could schedule me on Friday. I was devastated. I went home and told my Mother, and she said, "Oh, they told me the same thing at your age. Don't listen." So . . . I ignored the doctors and went about my artsy life; a little sad but grateful.

I performed in **Rent** (the Broadway musical), sang in packed nightclubs, and wrote a lot of poetry, trying to find my way to where I am now. I married my best friend when I was twenty-eight years old and for a while, things were going perfectly. My first album exploded, and I toured for two years straight. I made more money than I'd ever seen but overworked myself, almost to death. I realized that I had been putting too much of myself into working, and my body was telling me to refocus my energy. I "decided" that I was ready to have a baby. I went to see an endocrinologist about my absent period and was told the same thing: I wouldn't be having children and I should get a hysterectomy.

Honestly, I was still grateful for not having a cycle. I didn't miss the pain, but no baby? Ever? I went to my Mom and my Aunt in tears. They held me. My Aunt said, "Oooooh don't you worry 'bout that. You're going to have a fat thigh baby boy." I figured I should just reconcile with my current reality and move on. **Doctors know what they're talking about, right?**

I was grieving but holding steady when my husband of five years and I parted ways. (A new life in the entertainment industry can take its toll. Shame.) The night after I got the email saying that my divorce was final, I miraculously got my cycle. From that point on, I had a cycle every other month; not clockwork but a cycle nonetheless. It was like my body was saying maybe.

I started seeing a guy. We felt like a good match. My new boo and I planned a future together. He knew I couldn't have children but he had three and was willing to "share" with me. We were hopeful for a change, tho. In Mexico, in a **temazcal,** we prayed. We even discussed a family crest. We got engaged. No baby.

Time passed. I turned thirty-seven and was on my way to Botswana to shoot **The No. 1 Ladies' Detective Agency** for HBO. I was packing like crazy for a flight that left in a few hours. I hadn't been feeling well so I thought I'd see a doctor before I traveled to the Mother Continent. I was excited for the great acting opportunity. I was thrilled to tell the story of Precious Ramotswe and be #1 on the call sheet but I was constantly exhausted, easily sleeping for eleven hours each night. One sleep stretched for seventeen hours. Chile . . . I thought I had Cancer. What else could it be? I was worried. What would happen to my dreams? My life?

As I was throwing clothes and shoes into my bag, my phone rang. It was my doctor's office. I wasn't sick at all, I was pregnant. Whaaa????? I was in shock. After so many prayers, I was going to have my own baby. My Mother and Aunt's prediction was right. Still, I had to get myself together. I had a plane to catch.

I made it to Botswana and went to WORK, honey. We shot upwards of fifteen hours a day in one-hundred-degree heat. Every smell made me feel sick. Everyone on set had paper bags at-the-ready, from the camera crew to catering, because they never knew what was gonna make me throw up or when it would happen. I worked on. One scary day, a few months into my pregnancy, my ankles swelled and my skin turned gray. My doctor told me that I needed to take a few days off. I said, in tears, "I can't do that, I'm #1, everybody's counting on me." He said, "Whose baby is this?" The question hit me like a bag of bricks. I said, "Mine." He answered, "Exactly. You have to take care of **your baby**." It was a wake-up call. I realized that there was nobody else who could advocate for, and take care of, this little person I wanted so deeply. Collectively my cast and crew made key changes. I finished shooting at seven months pregnant.

After Africa, at seven and three-quarters months pregnant, I moved to California alone. My relationship didn't survive the shock of the unexpected pregnancy. When we were still together, we'd picked out a house and some furnishings. We had a plan. Then he informed me, after I moved, that he wasn't coming. I was devastated because I'd bought a house, because I dreamed of swimming naked with our baby in the sun, because I never ever imagined being a single parent. I was fucked up but carried on with the move. I had a very lonely time. It was absurd that I had all this love growing inside me and no one to share it with. It definitely felt like something irreplaceable was missing. I also didn't know anyone in California and my Mother couldn't come because she was taking care of my Blu. I wished I hadn't moved. I wished I shared this baby with someone who loved and cared for us but it was what it was.

Stuck in Cali (pregnant women can't fly after eight months), I asked God for help. My new community showed up with love and kindness. They didn't know me from Lucy but they went grocery shopping for us and took out my trash. My real estate agent introduced me to a kind heart named Lisa. Lisa helped me with the baby's room. Mo'Nique and sometimes Kym Whitley dropped from the sky and took me to a doctor's visit. They were all angels who I can never thank enough.

In my last month of pregnancy, I worked on making a home and I swam a lot. I kept thinking, **I'm going to be naked in this pool with my healthy baby soon. That's all I want to do.**

For my labor, I made a thirty-six-hour playlist. Labor wasn't "supposed" to last that long but I kept putting in music for different moods. And you know what? I ended up being in labor for exactly thirty-six hours. The doctors were concerned about pre-eclampsia so they induced; I think that's why it took so damn long. Ultimately, labor was pretty miraculous. By my bed, I had my dear friend (who I had helped give birth eight years prior), the ex (who was being "nice"), my doula, Ashley, and the doctor. For fifteen hours, I worked to get my baby out with no medication. It was getting pretty rough, so finally I asked for an epidural, but it didn't make the pain go away. Instead, my legs and feet just felt uncomfortably numb. At thirty-five and a half hours of labor, the doctor told me it was time for a Cesarean. I was thinking, **the fuck it is!** If I was going to get a Cesarean, it should've happened at least twenty hours ago. How could I have gone through all this, just to have a Cesarean at the end?

I said, "Wait, give me a minute." I thought of my Mother, who can heal with touch; my Aunt, who can see the future. I thought of **Wild Seed,** written by Octavia Butler. The character in the book was able to heal her body by going inside of herself, finding what was wrong, and then focusing on it to address it. I con-cen-trated, used my mind's eye to see my cervix, and I felt it open wide. I said, "Ok, now check." The doctor said, "You're fully dilated. Let's push."

In that moment, I was connected with the women in my family, and I didn't even know it. Blu was in the last month of her life; my Mother was dutifully at her side. In all the newness, fear, excitement, I didn't tell my Mom I was in labor but she knew anyway. My Mother told me that Blu had started to say, "push, push, push," in a faint voice randomly through the night. We were far apart, but somehow still together.

I pushed twelve times. The first couple of times, I was so tired that I wasn't truly present. My doctor recognized this and put my hand between my legs. I felt something that wasn't me. I started to focus again. I saw Fern, the dog my Mom had when I was a kid. I remembered Fern giving birth to a litter of puppies, how focused she was, and how calm. She didn't yelp or moan. She just did this faraway breathing thing. It was beautiful. I remember my Mom telling me, "Don't scream while pushing. When you inhale hard you suck the baby back up. Just focus. Your body knows what it's meant to do." So I breathed like Fern. I didn't scream, like Mom said, I believed, I prayed, and I welcomed a healthy dream into the world and yes, THANK YOU, GOD, we swam naked every day for a good long while.

Chosen Family
JENNIE JEDDRY AND KIM DELISE
Camera Operator and Filmmaker

JENNIE: I would call it love at first sight. We're both in film and we met on a job in 2005 out in the Hamptons, where the crew lived together in these old mansions—like sleepaway camp. I remember first seeing Kim in the bathroom, when I was wearing these ridiculous pink polyester grandpa pants—a late 1990s style statement for queer feminist punk musicians—and brushing my teeth. She walked in and I felt an electric jolt of nervousness.

KIM: It was . . . strange.

JENNIE: So strange. We connected romantically right away. Then we were assigned to share a room—a room with a luxurious king-sized bed and a tiny, rickety cot. And, well, that was that. We took the bed.

KIM: We had **zero** conversations about family or children early on in our relationship.

JENNIE: I suppose I relate to the word "parent" more than the word "mother." When I was a kid, I was very into the idea of being a parent; I always had baby dolls. My mom was a single mother, and I really respected her. Looking back, I think I was so into caring for my "babies" because I wanted to be taken care of in that way. But then, as a queer person, in my teens and twenties, the thought of having kids of my own never entered my mind. I didn't know any queer people who had kids, and I really thought of my community as my "family." I had my **chosen** family. I was focused on my life with my friends in New York, playing with my band, and fighting for queer liberation. The idea of traditional family almost felt counterrevolutionary.

KIM: In Italian-American culture, family comes before everything, and that's what I grew up in. When I was a kid, I thought I wanted children because I assumed that is just what you do, it was what was expected of me. But as I got older and came into my own, I started to question what I **really** wanted from life. My mother was wholly steeped in her identity of motherhood; she found her value entirely in being a mother. I recognized that I did not want it to consume me. I wanted to have a career. I wanted to maintain my sense of self, and my ambitions.

It was a few years into our relationship when the subject of kids came up, one night when we were walking along the beach under a full moon while we were camping in Puerto Rico.

JENNIE: We had been spending time with our nieces, and I just loved seeing Kim with them—she didn't quite know what to do with kids, but they loved her. And I thought, **I want this.** It wasn't exactly like a switch went off; it was more like the pilot light had always been there and suddenly, the burner came back on. And still, today, one of the most joyful things in my life is watching Kim interact with our children.

KIM: Jennie's the type who's like, **Okay, let's do this.** And I was more hesitant, I needed some time.

JENNIE: So we took five years. When we decided it was time, we quickly came to the conclusion that Kim would carry. She's a few years older than me, so we thought it'd be smart to have her go first. But also, I'm a Steadicam operator, and it's an incredibly physically demanding job. It would have been impossible to do while pregnant.

We went to a fertility doctor and decided we wanted our donor to be anonymous. The first thing the clinic required us to do was go to a therapy session, which ended up being incredibly valuable, because it helped us to think clearly about the whole process, and it gave us tools for how to talk to our kid about how they were born; how to give them the language and story from the beginning so they don't make up their own and wonder, **Where's my dad?**

KIM: After an IUI that didn't take and one miscarriage, a pregnancy took. I went to a birthing center for my prenatal care. I wanted to go full throttle into the experience—give birth in a tub and all that. But the center had a rule that you couldn't give birth past forty-one weeks and six days, so when I went past my due date, I was anxious. Finally, at exactly forty-one weeks and six days, I went into labor. I was so grateful that I could still go to the birthing center. But when we got there, the baby's heart rate was dropping with each contraction, and they didn't have the ability to safely monitor something like that. So, within fifteen minutes of arriving, we were in an ambulance, headed to the hospital.

Luckily, the midwife was able to go with us, and we got straight into a room. The doctors were aligned with my midwife's philosophies. They encouraged me to keep laboring without intervention, and I did, for hours and hours, but the heart rate continued to drop. It was probably harder on Jennie because the whole time I was doing hypnobirthing, which I had practiced during pregnancy. I was in a **zone.**

JENNIE: She was amazing! The doctors asked, "What kind of drugs is she on?" She hadn't had anything.

KIM: But I labored for a long time, and was beyond exhausted. Eventually, I got the epidural and some Pitocin to help my cervix open up. After forty-eight hours I finally got to nine and a half centimeters, but the baby's heart rate kept dropping dramatically and the doctor said, "I'm very concerned. You start to push right now, it's going to be dangerous." So, we made a collective decision to go with the emergency C-section. And at the time I was relieved. I thought, **Okay, this feels right.**

JENNIE: The surgery went well. They pulled Émile out and he was perfect. The drop in heart rate turned out to be his umbilical cord being pressed up against Kim's pelvis as he descended. They put a little heart sticker on his chest for the monitor leads. I'd never seen someone so beautiful. He had Kim's feet! I got to go over and see him when they were cleaning him up. And that was the moment—immediately I thought, **That's my son.** I wasn't quite sure what I was going to feel, since it was all new territory for me, and I wasn't the birth mother. But there was no question, no hesitation. We did skin-on-skin contact while they were sewing Kim up, and it was the most remarkable feeling. Our bond was strong.

KIM: Although I came out of surgery feeling initially good, and I felt like we made the right decisions, and that I had done everything I could, it definitely took me years to deal with that feeling of failing in some way, for not having a vaginal birth. It was hard. I didn't get my unmedicated water birth. I didn't get my tub!

And after that, things didn't immediately ease up. I didn't have any sort of lack of love for my son, but I did feel trapped by the postpartum experience— breastfeeding constantly (and not enjoying it as much as I'd hoped I would) while trying to recover from this massive battle wound from birth. It was so much to handle, and I was putting a lot of pressure on myself. I was never diagnosed, but I believe I dealt with some degree of postpartum depression. It was a slow process of reclaiming myself—or, my new sense of self.

JENNIE: We had this incredibly liberating moment when we finally switched to formula, about seven months in. We cared about the benefits of breast-feeding, but ultimately, we both accepted that our son was going to be on formula now, and that was okay. It was suddenly clear that our mental health was more important than breastfeeding. Being in a good place mentally was the most important thing for us and for our baby—for everyone. If we were stressed out trying to do things "perfectly" and it wasn't working and we were not getting along, that wouldn't be good for Émile either.

Kim and I both strongly feel that motherhood **cannot** be giving up on yourself. It just cannot. Whatever it takes, our own self-care has to be part of it, or we'll go crazy. Trying to be a mother while you're completely drained is . . . it's just too much.

KIM: After things stabilized a few years in, we decided we were ready to have another.

JENNIE: It was my turn. I was so excited. I was in a more established place in my career, so I could afford to step back from Steadicam operating. For those of us who work physical jobs, whether it's athletics or work that simply doesn't go hand in hand with pregnancy, carrying a baby is a challenge. It's a challenge for anyone, of course, but for those of us with physically demanding careers, we simply **can't** do our jobs while pregnant. My Steadicam vest is metal, the whole rig weighs about fifty pounds, and is fitted to my non-pregnant torso—and that's that. I could still work as a camera operator, luckily, but that was approximately a 50 percent pay cut. So, I lost half my income, but it was worth it to me. We are privileged; many people don't have the financial freedom to make that choice.

On my third try I got pregnant, in November of 2020, with the same sperm donor we had used for Émile. I had some health risks that needed to be monitored, so I decided to give birth at a hospital with a doula. It just felt right; the hospital is by the river, and water's been an important part of our relationship, so that felt auspicious.

Because I was thirty-nine years old and I didn't want to be induced (without a good reason for induction), the doctor had me come in every day after I reached my due date. At forty-one weeks and two days I went in and they saw that the baby's heart rate was decelerating intermittently. The doctor said, "You need to go to the hospital to be induced **now**." I had a dream of a long labor at home with my doula—that was gone in an instant.

KIM: We didn't have anything with us! I had to go home and get the bag. I was like, "Okay, I guess I'll see you at the hospital?"

JENNIE: I remember being on an empty train, with just my wallet and a smoothie. And I thought, **Okay, I am not in control anymore. Here we go.** I got out of the subway, and, I don't like hospitals in general, but I looked at that hospital where I'd be having my baby and I thought, **That is a sparkling beacon of hope!** My doula met me there, and she brought a rock from the beach in Normandy, where she is from. My grandfather, who was turning one hundred that year, had been at D-Day on that beach, so it was meaningful to me. Everything just felt right, even though it was scary. I held the rock as I labored, with Kim and my doula (and a rotation of incredibly loving and skilled nurses) by my side, and everything was amazing, even though it was, of course, **intense.** I thought about ten minutes had passed . . .

KIM: No, it was the whole night. It was twelve hours.

JENNIE: Twelve hours later, I had finally made it to eight centimeters dilated, and they told me I'd be pushing soon, and we all were excited. But then something changed. I started vomiting everywhere, and I felt searing pain. It didn't feel right. My doula asked, "Are you in pain because it's labor, or are you **suffering?**" I looked at her with tears running down my face and told her I was suffering. I knew what labor felt like, and this was different. I asked for a walking epidural, which meant that it would wear off by the time it came to push, and I could still walk around. An epidural wasn't in my original birth plan, but we all agreed it would be the most self-loving thing I could do at that moment, and my doula and Kim reminded me that things **change**, that I could pivot, and that there was no reason I had to suffer.

KIM: They did an ultrasound, and we saw that the baby was sunny-side up; he was jammed up on one side of her pelvis, and the pain she was feeling was back labor. They started talking about a C-section.

JENNIE: And my brilliant doula, who is trained in the "spinning babies" technique, asked the doctor if she could just have thirty minutes to try to get the baby to move. Using this scarf, she and Kim worked **hard** for twenty minutes, shimmying the scarf around me to get the baby to move down. And then—this was one of the best moments of my life—I felt this shift, like a fish swimming down, and all the pain went away. My doula said, "He flipped. You're good." It was the sweetest relief. And then it was time to push.

KIM: Twenty-seven hours into labor, Jennie was pretty tired. In sixteen years, I'd never seen her that tired. Then, the hospital shifts changed, and this beautiful, energetic, trans woman nurse came in and really kicked the room into gear.

JENNIE: She looked right at me and said, "You're beautiful. You're strong. And I think we need some music."

KIM: She put on nineties aerobics music, because that's what gets Jennie going. And when "Rhythm Is a Dancer" by Snap! came on, Jennie let it rip (literally) and Marcel shot out.

JENNIE: After that, it was a dream. This wild, intense storm kicked in, and we were just snuggled with our beautiful newborn on the thirteenth floor. Our older son was safe with his grandparents, and we just watched the rain pour down. It was blissful.

KIM: After having given birth, it was just the most amazing thing to get to witness it. When you're the one birthing, you can just be so inside yourself. So, to get to be fully present with what was happening was a miracle. I feel like I finally fully arrived, confident in my identity as a parent when Marcel was born. Émile, the son I had given birth to, was five years old—but now I felt like a parent!

I think we've both been tremendously changed by parenthood. In one way, you have to set yourself aside, because these little beings have so many needs. But in another way, you learn that you can **never** give up on yourself, because in order to take care of someone else, you **must** be in a good place. It's a delicate, constant balancing act.

JENNIE: Yes, and we've both discovered that this job is something we cannot do alone—we need help. And that help can come in many forms, whether it's friends or therapy or simple acts of self-care. It's part of the reason Kim and I chose to raise our children in the city—a sense of community and support is supremely important to us.

KIM: We have people who we hire as babysitters, but we also have a roster of friends, neighbors, and family that we can call on when we're in a bind. We both love having a larger community to rely on, to be held by. And it feels good that our sons have these aunties and grandparents and people around that they know and feel comfortable with.

JENNIE: And that's our chosen family too. Before we decided we wanted a family that looked like this—two children and two parents—we valued our family in our creative communities, in our queer communities, in our music communities, our film communities. And now our children's families are those communities. As their parents, we want to be a huge, important part of our kids' lives, but we also want them to be raised and loved by many people. Each person has something particular and valuable to offer our sons, and being able to enrich our kids' lives in that way—to help them feel supported and empowered to find family wherever it feels right—means the world to us.

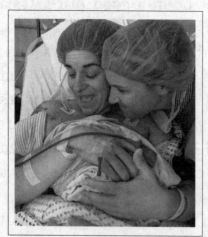
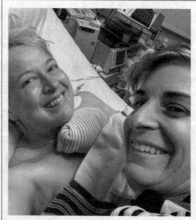

What Works for YOU

LA LA ANTHONY

Actress

The pregnancy was a surprise. Carmelo and I were serious about our commitment to one another, but we'd never even talked about having kids. I was chasing my career in entertainment, and he was chasing basketball, playing for the Denver Nuggets. I come from a big Puerto Rican family in Brooklyn, but I didn't feel any pressure to have kids. I figured that if it was meant to be, babies would come later.

When I found out I was pregnant, I was a host on **Total Request Live (TRL)**, a music-video show that catered to teens. I thought MTV would replace me right away. How's it going to look, me, with this big belly, on TV? I was twenty-five and unmarried. I worried about the optics, but I also wasn't sure if I could pull off the logistics of being a working mom.

This was sixteen years ago, which might not sound that long ago, but a lot has changed in sixteen years. Back then, there wasn't childcare or a playroom set up at work, none of the stuff that you see on movie or TV sets now. Of course, there were working moms everywhere, but the kids were nowhere to be seen.

I kept the pregnancy to myself as long as I could, but from the first few weeks on, I suffered from hyperemesis. I was sick **all** the time, throwing up, barely eating, and just miserable. There was no history of this in my family; my mom has always said that she had the best pregnancies ever. MTV asked me to host the red carpet at the 2006 **VMAs**, and I knew I'd never make it through that event without puking on somebody's dress, so I had to tell them. I was so scared, but they were incredibly supportive. I can thank my fan base for that—they loved me on the show. But I'm still grateful to MTV because they could've said, "A baby out of wedlock isn't the message we want to send to kids," and let me go.

Carmelo and I saw the pregnancy as a blessing, not a burden. But the question was: How would we navigate it? We weren't even living together; he was in Denver, and I was shooting in New York. I had been flying back and forth between the two cities, and that wasn't going to work anymore. Eventually, I took my leave from MTV and settled in Denver with Melo a couple of months before I was due.

But before I left, I had to shoot the rest of **TRL**

in the worst condition of my life. Hyperemesis is so debilitating, you literally feel like you're dying. I would throw up, on average, nine times a day. It was that bad. I only gained maybe fifteen pounds my entire pregnancy. Every day I shot on **TRL**, I would tell myself, "Just make it to the commercial break." And without fail, every break, I'd be in the back throwing up—everyone could see it. Then it was like, "Drink some water. Brush your teeth real quick. And get back out there."

I kept waiting for the sickness to let up, but it only got worse from there. Some women only have hyperemesis for the first trimester. That passed, then so did months five, six, and seven with absolutely no relief. I was always telling myself that I just had to make it one more day, and then another, and another. My doctor told me it was one of the worst cases she'd ever seen.

Throughout all of this, I was terrified; there is a high incidence of miscarriage when you have hyperemesis. Early in month seven, I was rushed to the hospital because I was having contractions. They gave me a shot of steroids to help the baby's lungs mature, and tried their best to hold off labor. At this point, my son weighed only three pounds.

Miraculously, I avoided going into full labor and was sent home, after celebrating New Year's Eve in the hospital, with a lit candle on my hospital dinner tray. I wasn't put on strict bed rest, but I was so sick that I couldn't do anything else anyway. I had to have an IV PICC line set up at my house, to keep me hydrated. At thirty-six weeks, with my amniotic fluid low, my doctor said the baby was healthy enough to come out. I really don't know how much longer I could've taken the mental and physical stress.

I never got to experience the excitement and joy of being pregnant. When women say they love being pregnant, I just can't imagine that feeling. My life was at a standstill. If I wasn't on TV, I was just curled up sick somewhere. I didn't even have a baby shower. That pregnancy is why, I think, subconsciously and consciously, I've only ever had one child. I'm too terrified to ever go through something like that again.

I was blessed with an easy birth, though. My doctor induced me when the baby weighed five pounds, nine ounces, so it was easy to get him out. I just looked at him in awe when he was finally in my arms. When I'd gone on chat rooms for hyper-emesis, the women there would say, "One day, this little human will thank you." And of course, he didn't understand it that day, but he does now. And in that instant, holding him for the first time, nine months seemed like the smallest sacrifice to make. He was this great, healthy kid—still is. I had reached the light at the end of the tunnel, at last.

Once he was out, it was like a switch: I just didn't throw up anymore. I had gone from only small bites of dry waffles back to regular eating again. Someone in my family was like, "OK, what do you want to eat?" And I asked them to bring me steak and lobster, the most obnoxious meal I could think of. They brought it into the hospital and I was actually able to eat it and keep it down. It was the most fascinating thing, after nine months, to suddenly be able to chew, digest, and enjoy food again. I realized how much I had taken for granted before. I'll never forget that incredible meal; it almost didn't feel real.

After the hyperemesis vanished, I was ready to tackle whatever motherhood threw my way. I was healthy. I had my energy back. The usual postpartum struggles, the lack of sleep and all that, just didn't phase me. I was just so happy to not be sick. I was like, **I'll stay up for three days straight as long as I don't throw up!**

We were young parents; Melo had just turned twenty-two, and we had so much to figure out, so much to learn about what kind of parents we would be. From the first night I brought my son home from the hospital, I learned that I was a protective parent. I stayed up all night just watching him breathe. Melo told me to go to bed but I was like, "What if he stops?"

We named our son Kiyan Carmelo Anthony. At the time, there were a lot of other basketball players having babies and one of the other parents said to me, in kind of a nasty way, "I can't believe you wouldn't name him Carmelo Jr." But I didn't want that for him; I didn't want him walking around with the weight of that name on him. His dad's name is, of course, still in there, but Kiyan gets to be his own person.

Motherhood is not knowing what you're doing and figuring it out along the way. There's no manual and each kid is different. You can get advice from others but ultimately, it's about what works for **you**. Nothing proved this more to me than when Kiyan was having digestion issues when he was almost two years old.

He always cried after drinking his formula or any liquids. At first, I thought it must be the formula so I switched to brand after brand, but no matter what we tried, something was still bothering him. I took him to a doctor who said he was fine. Even people in my family, and friends, were like, "He's fine, you're overreacting," but I knew I wasn't. So I took him to more doctors, and it turned out he had a kidney issue and needed surgery. There was a blockage somewhere and his kidneys weren't flushing properly.

The surgery he needed was a big deal. I'll never forget seeing my baby under anesthesia, and how out of it he was when he woke up. He came home after being in the hospital for a few days, and thankfully, recovered into a fully healthy and active kid. It was one of those experiences that proved to me that you can get all the smart advice in the world from experienced parents—from doctors, even—but if your gut is telling you something different, you have to shut out all the outside noise and tune in to your own instincts.

When I was little, I never thought that my mother was winging it, ever. She had the answers to everything. **What do I do if I'm sick? What do I do for my hair?** I still ask her for advice on major career decisions and even though she's not in the entertainment business, she will give me the simplest answer that immediately makes everything clear. Parents have a way of cutting through the bullshit like that.

To this day, my mom is my best friend, but it wasn't until I was an adult that I realized that her answers were, and are, based on her upbringing and her experiences in life. My mom is proud of me, but she can't help but tell me things like, "Don't work too hard," and ask, "Don't you just want to stay home sometimes?" She was a single mom who worked full-time; maybe she wished she could've stayed home more for my brother and me. I try to explain to her that leaning out of my career wouldn't make me happy.

Still, the demands of my work and Carmelo's are hard. All of my career decisions have to sync with being a parent. I'm lucky that **Power** shot in Brooklyn for six seasons, and then **The Chi** was in Chicago, which was an easy flight from New York, but what about the next show? Kiyan's fifteen, he's not going to want to just pick up and go to Vancouver, if I booked something there. I would never leave him, so he has to come wherever I go.

With Carmelo's career, it's even tougher. For Kiyan, it's a strange contradiction: The whole world is happy because your dad's playing for a certain team, but you just want your father home with you. Carmelo left New York when Kiyan was around eleven to play for the Oklahoma City Thunder and it was rough on all of us. Not too long after, Carmelo and I separated but stayed close. Right now, in quarantine, we're actually all together at Melo's house in Portland. Kiyan has been in heaven: He loves having his parents back under one roof again. It's been fun, but let's see if it's still working in a week or two!

For most of his life, Kiyan has lived in New York, which is the center of my family. I grew up with lots of cousins, aunts, and uncles always dropping by the house. It's important to me that he understands his African-American and Puerto Rican roots through living it: having his cousins over all the time, eating Spanish food, dancing at every party. New York kids just understand diversity because it's everywhere. That said, there are still risks to the city, you have to be careful. And of course, this applies to the world at large: I've talked at length with Kiyan about what being a young

Black man in America means. We talked about Trayvon Martin's murder, and how to deal with police. He understands that he doesn't have the same privileges that another kid might have.

Kiyan is also a basketball player, and as of fall 2021, he's playing for Christ the King High School in Queens, which has turned out several NBA players. Scouts for college teams and the NBA are already watching him. At tournaments, kids and even parents will say terrible things to him, like how he won't ever be as good as his dad—and that's just the PG-rated version. Kiyan lets all those dumb comments roll right off his back. He says, "Mom, I'm not even thinking about that stuff, it doesn't bother me." I always tell him that he doesn't have to play basketball . . . that we're going to support and love him no matter who he is.

He has such a chill, laid-back personality, like his dad, but I've always made it clear to Kiyan that he can talk to me about **anything**. I never want to be the parent who's checked out, who has no idea what her kid is listening to or experiencing in the world. Whatever hip hop he's into, I know all the songs and the words.

I don't get the concept of "I'm either your mother or your friend but I can't be both." I don't think it has to be one or the other. I can still make sure that he doesn't spend too much time playing video games, while also being there for him as a friend and confidante. That's what I most want for our future: for us to stay close. For him to feel like he can talk to me about anything without judgment. He'll know that he's going to get honest advice, honest answers, nothing sugar-coated. I'm not going to just tell him what he wants to hear; I'm **always** going to tell him the truth.

The Birth of a Blended Family
SHEA WILLIAMS
Business Owner

When I was seventeen, my seemingly perfect life exploded into pieces. A few months before his death at thirty-nine, my involved and devoted dad, who loved coaching me in sports, morphed into a quietly hostile figure who only communicated with my brother. He wouldn't speak to my sister, my mother, or me. Diabetes 1, with which he'd been diagnosed years earlier, had taken its toll on his health but his personality shift was still inexplicable, and incredibly painful for all of us. Then he was found dead of a heart attack in a hotel room, in a different state, with no ID on him and $3,000 in cash. It looked like he was trying to leave the family and start a new life but we'll never know the full story.

His death cast a shadow over my desire to have children. My mother and grandmother, both huge influences on me, described birth and motherhood as empowering and beautiful. But would it be that way for me? My personality was a lot like my father's, so I worried that when I reached his age, I'd fall prey to the same mysterious demons and abandon my children, either by death or depression. How could I bring a child into this world knowing that I could possibly hurt her as much as my dad's death had hurt me?

Grief and anger led to a few lost years of heavy drinking and partying as I tried to run from any chance of love appearing in my life. By age twenty-six, though, things were turning around. I was hiking every day in Los Angeles, where I was living after a nomadic summer with my boyfriend, Remy. I felt in touch with my true desires, and somehow, I knew that I was going to have a child soon, even if our relationship was hitting the rocks.

I wasn't on birth control when my daughter Levi was conceived several months later, shortly after I moved back to my home state, Ohio. At the time, there were two guys in my life: My now ex-boyfriend, Remy, who had come from L.A. to get me back, and a local fling who I didn't see a future with at all. In the middle of this horrible love triangle, I found myself staring at a positive pregnancy test. If it had been a couple of years earlier, I may not have kept the pregnancy, and even as it was, I called a clinic to look into my options. Ultimately, my intuition led me to having this baby.

I wasn't sure who my daughter's father was but when an OB told me the likely date of conception, I did the math and figured it was Remy. After a brief stint in Florida, where Levi was born, the three of us eventually moved to Chicago to start a life together, to varying degrees of success. The big obstacle: The older Levi got, the clearer it became that Remy wasn't her biological father. I'd thrown myself into life with Levi head-first, but the uncertainty and de facto deception of the situation with Remy made me sick with stress. I wanted to prevent hurting her (and him) as much as possible, but if I wanted to be honest, I had no choice.

Since my life had been destroyed by my dad's death, I wanted Levi's to be perfect. I wanted to be a great mother who never faltered, who would always be there for her. But there is no such thing as perfect, really. You can have the most enviable nuclear family, and it can all be shattered in an instant. Nothing is guaranteed. What I didn't know yet was that shattering is sometimes the only path forward, not to a perfect life but to something hard-won and honest.

Eventually, I told Remy about my suspicions, and a DNA test soon confirmed them. Telling him the truth was the hardest experience of my adult life so far. Our romantic connection was never great but we had always been close friends underneath it all. I never wanted to hurt him like that.

About a year later, I told my daughter, who was not even three years old. I explained that she'd always have him in her life but that he wasn't her biological father. "Biological" wasn't a word she was familiar with but I knew she'd eventually understand. I believe that you can tell a child a lot of things and what they're ultimately reading are your emotional cues: Are you grounded and balanced as you're telling them? If so, that's what they'll remember, and that's what gives them a sense of stability. Her biological father, by the way, chose not to become her legal parent, but Remy, who's now married, still has a good relationship with Levi.

After the breakup, Levi and I got our own apartment in Chicago, which I could finally afford because of a new nanny job, a small stream of income from my just-launched photography business, and a part-time waitressing gig. Two of these jobs gave me the freedom to keep my child with me while I made money. Through this transition, I always emphasized to her that our rock-solid bond would get us through whatever happened next—although I had no idea what that would be.

During those years, I would sometimes say to friends, "Things are crazy right now but I have a feeling that when I'm thirty-three, I'll have another kid." I was mostly just throwing a number out there, but intuition was right again: I was thirty-two and living back in Ohio when I met a reserved guy named Jay on Bumble. I knew immediately he was the one. We went on our first date in October and I got pregnant in December; we conceived our daughter Maren on my thirty-third birthday.

Jay already had two daughters, a three-year-old and a six-year-old, and we had planned to slowly introduce our children over the next few months. Obviously, the pregnancy threw a wrench into those plans. I came over after his youngest daughter's birthday party to tell him the news. We both just sat with our eyes wide open, unsure whether to laugh, cry, or celebrate. By the time I woke up the next morning, he had a list of local midwives, and we resolved to figure it out together.

By February, we were all living together in one big, blended family. The girls get along well, but of course there have been hiccups, tantrums, and fights along the way. It's hard on all of us. With your own kids, there's a built-in promise: Levi knows that when I'm mad at her, I still love her and I'm not going anywhere. But when I have to discipline the other girls, it's more delicate. They're also half-time at their mom's, so the composition and dynamics of our house changes from day to day. It's hard to find equilibrium in a mixed family, and if anyone says it's not, they're lying.

Levi has also had to learn how to share me. During the days when I was pregnant, she'd be playful and sweet, but at night when we were alone, she'd whisper, "I don't want you to have another baby." Her secret feelings set off shame within myself. I couldn't believe I'd gotten pregnant by accident again. Like, what is wrong with me? How did this happen? (Well, okay, I knew how: I had developed a latex allergy after my first pregnancy, and Jay and I hadn't been able to find condoms we liked, so we sometimes didn't use them. Plus, I don't think either of us were too hell-bent on not having a baby together.)

This time, I knew who the father was and that I loved him, but it was still hard. I didn't have time to process what was happening; I just had to **go go go** so that our lives could smoothly merge. Ultimately, I knew this new reality would be good for Levi and me but it came at us so fast and furious. Suddenly, I was co-parenting three very active kids, two of them near strangers, while also waitressing, selling Beautycounter products, and trying to give my new relationship the time and attention it deserved. At 3 P.M. on some days, I'd look up and realize I hadn't eaten anything yet.

I was so harried that, despite dreaming of giving birth with the legendary midwife Ina May Gaskin on her Tennessee farm, I settled for a home birth with a midwife with whom I'd never really clicked. I'm convinced that made the birth physically harder for me; a woman's emotional context can change the process of laboring. If the wrong people are in the room, you literally can't open up, which is what you need to do to get that baby out of there!

On September 10, at forty-one weeks, I finally went into labor around 6 P.M. I spent part of those early hours rocking in Jay's arms in the kitchen, anchored by his warmth. Then the midwife, Nicole, came to our house with six people, not exactly the intimate experience I craved. They draped my living room in protective plastic sheets; we settled in for a long night. Eventually the contractions became super painful: They surged through my entire body, leaving me quivering in their wake. I was going to die, I was sure of it. I hadn't expected the birth to be so difficult; Levi's had gone so smoothly. Nicole told me to get into child's pose, which is when you sit on your knees and fold over so that your forehead is touching the floor, but I laid my head in Jay's lap. She then instructed me to hold my breath while I pushed because that makes the push more effective, but it was painful. As I was struggling to catch my breath, Jay bent down and whispered in my ear, "Baby, you're doing so good. We are so close to meeting her. You can do this, but you've got to hold your breath and push. She's right there, baby."

I caught an urgency in his voice, but what I didn't know was that Maren had just passed meconium in the womb. If swallowed or inhaled, meconium can cause serious problems. I gathered enough energy to hold a deep breath and push with all my might. Her head started to crown and then slip back; **she was**

right there! I went deep inside myself: My vagina might be blown to smithereens but I decided I would push two more times and she would be out. Another super-sized contraction came and I gave it every ounce of energy I had to push with my mouth sealed shut. As her head broke the barrier between the womb and the world, I screamed louder than I've ever screamed in my life. It was equal parts pain and satisfaction. After one more contraction, she was all the way out.

Maren was very gray, and she didn't cry right away. She didn't swallow any meconium, but she had swallowed a lot of other fluid that needed to be suctioned out before she could take her first breath. Time ceased to move as the midwife worked to get her airways clear. There was no past and no future, just this moment. It was a mini eternity until Maren finally took her first breath. With her wail, my life started again.

While I pushed her out, I thought: **In this moment, there are millions of women with me.** There are millions who have come before me, and millions more will come after. Having children made me more interested in taking care of other women, particularly other mothers. My sister has two kids, and we talk about this a lot, how there are these moments when only another mother knows what you need—a warm meal or someone to just hold your baby while you shower, the simple things.

I expected my postpartum experience with Maren

to be easier than with Levi because I had a loving partner now to help me out. Instead, it was harder. Once she was born, I grappled with the enormous changes of the last nine months. I had these three big kids and this husband, and they all needed me too. It was a tough reckoning. Levi was so sad that our lengthy bedtime routine had to change. I'd cry at night, thinking, **How can I give her what she needs? Am I in over my head? How am I ever going to find balance?**

Breastfeeding helped. During the chaos of Maren's early months, it forced me into a quiet place where there was nothing I could do but lie down and connect with her. Everything else might feel like a disaster, but as long as my body could feed my baby, I was still a competent mom. You're competent if you solely use formula too, but for me, breastfeeding was a lifeline to a sense of calm and purpose.

I also made a conscious choice to be a different kind of parent. With Levi, I never let anyone else help but I wanted to be more flexible this time. Now I ask for help when I need it, which is good for the whole family. Maren is the only person in the house that's related to all of us, and in that way, she feels like the puzzle piece that made us fit as a set. For the kids, she's equally each girl's sister, and that helps them see that Jay and I are both equally their parents, and they are all equally our children.

On any given day, the energy in our house is electric and bouncing, and I wouldn't have it any other way. This messy, sweet family feels right to me. I'm built to roll with the punches; I thrive on the unexpected. I was never going to be the person with the cookie-cutter life, the nine-to-five job, the tidy little predictable marriage. Sometimes Jay and I talk about having another baby; we both really want a boy. Needless to say, it'll be a little crazy if we have another. For now, we're holding off. We've got enough chaos and joy to last us awhile.

Postscript: In May 2021, Shea and Jay welcomed their twin boys, Whitman and Asa.

How Rough and Beautiful

SIENNA MILLER

Actress

I've never been a particularly practical thing, in work or love. I'm a knee-jerk reaction come to life: impulsive, sometimes rash but always present in the moment. Of course I could take a more organized and structured approach to my life, but I've always been attracted to what's intuitive and creative. My philosophy has always been to let life figure itself out as you live it.

When I met my daughter's father at a tour of a Picasso exhibition, we clicked instantly as friends. He was hilarious and charming. For the next four years, we were in and out of each other's lives. Then one evening we had a drink and something new sparked. Two weeks later, he moved in. We almost immediately started trying to have a baby but we never sat down and made an official plan. What a thrill to just not be careful! After seven months, I was pregnant. The night we found out, we tore off to a birthday party and deliciously guarded the secret from everyone else. It's so special, that time when only the two of you know.

For all the freedom of the conception, the actual birth was extremely difficult, as well as the aftermath. My intuition didn't foretell how birthing and caring for a baby would crush up who I was and create a new woman in her place: a mother. From that point forward, nothing was ever the same. It took me two or three years to settle from the enormity of that shift.

When I was little, I didn't consider the emotional or physical labor of motherhood. I dove straight into the fantasy. Ah yes, here I am as an aged matriarch sitting at the head of a solid oak table, buttering a freshly baked loaf of bread, with children and grandchildren all bustling about. I didn't think about making endless meals and scrubbing floors and piles of laundry. I romanticized the idea of a big brood. Perhaps I wanted this robust clan because my own family was so different: We were quite an insular little unit. It was just me, my mum, who was this near-mythical force while I was growing up, and my older sister, who is my rock and still to this day my gold standard for female relationships.

In my twenties, I did experience the realities of child-rearing firsthand as a stepmom of sorts. My boyfriend had three children: a six-year-old, a three-year-old, and a ten-month-old. I was there for the early mornings, night feeds, and nappy changes. My sister was having children too. So I saw the day-to-day reality, but it's much easier to manage them when they're not your own. I could get my boyfriend's kids up and out the door for school, no problem, but my own daughter can be a struggle.

My first inkling that I was forging a new identity was in that first trimester when, for the first time in my life, I became a napper. It might sound small, but all my life I've struggled to take naps, and suddenly I couldn't get enough. When I went to South Africa to film **The Girl**, about Hitchcock's obsession with Tippi Hedren, I played the titular blonde through my fatigue. For the re-creation of **The Birds**, they put maggots and worms in my pockets to attract the birds that needed to flap in my face. Needless to say, I was miserable.

I finished filming at sixteen weeks and after a breezy second trimester, I entered the "house on legs" third. I had this enormous bump and I looked like I'd gotten my lips done. I could not stop eating sugar. I would convince myself, no matter what part of London I was driving through, that The

Hummingbird Bakery was on the way home and I'd swing by for red velvet cupcakes. A cabdriver once leaned out his window and shouted, "Not long, love," and I think I gave him the finger. Little did he know I was still weeks away.

My body was not my own and it showed in some of my auditions. For **August: Osage County,** I remember having to really cry and feeling guilty for putting my body, possibly my baby, through the experience. It made me anxious: Can your body tell the difference between acting and reality?

As we got closer, I wondered if I'd have anything like my sister's or my mother's births. My sister is the hypno-birthing doula queen, the type who has three orgasms while pushing and doesn't ever scream. My mother had both of us at thirty-seven weeks, but an early delivery wasn't my fate either. Instead, I found myself at forty-two weeks hiking to the top of St. Paul's Cathedral in the boiling July heat. By then, the doctors wanted to induce me but I said no, I would bring this on. People were horrified watching this waddling lump clambering up the incredibly narrow stairs. There are some photos of me where I thought I looked attractive, but my bump was actually obscuring an entire spire.

Late that night, after an uneventful dinner with our parents, we finally went to hospital to surrender to the induction plan. After the intake exam, the nurses said to me, "Do you know you're already having contractions?" They were coming every ten minutes and I couldn't feel it. To speed things along, they gave me some Pitocin gel, but I wish they hadn't. It made labor, which was already occurring naturally, violently accelerate. I had been up since seven in the morning and had climbed St. Paul's; I was exhausted. From there, it all started to go badly.

By 3 A.M., the contractions were rampant. To make things nice, we had electric candles burning, and I was still desperately hoping I'd get to deliver in the bath. My doctor came in at 6 A.M., and I was only two centimeters dilated. I refused an epidural because I was still clinging to the bath dream. I was inhaling gas and trying to ride the waves but twelve hours later, still with no sleep, and the baby's back pressing into my spine, I was worn down. In came the epidural and more Pitocin.

After more than twenty-six hours in the hospital, I finally reached full dilation. I was pushing and couldn't feel anything. And then our baby's heart rate started to dip. Halfway through a contraction, the doctor ran out of the room. The midwife tried to console me, told me to keep going. "What's happening?" I kept asking. By then the doctor had returned—in scrubs.

He said, "We're just going to take you into the operating room, just in case, but everything is all right." Suddenly, Tom was in scrubs too. The baby's heart rate kept plummeting with every contraction. The doctor took out the ventouse and anchored his foot on the end of my bed as he tried to suction the baby out. The muscles in his leg were pumping as he was angling and struggling to get her out but she had moved positions. It wasn't working. Real alarm set in.

Doctors rushed in and the next thing I knew, I was being pumped with drugs in preparation for an emergency C-section. They took a syringe of water and kept squirting some on my stomach. "Can you feel it?" Finally, I was numb, but due to the influx of drugs, I suppose, I started convulsing. It was all a blur but I could feel my body thrashing. The doctors were now racing to get me out of surgery, to get this all over with. By that time I had been awake for forty hours and was barely cognizant. The room was a haze of images: Tom, ghostly white. My sister was a face in the door, weeping. I think they thought I was going to die. My own thoughts weren't anything but **Get her out. Get her out now.**

Then, in the midst of this harrowing situation, she arrived. Marlowe, in full scream. After this ordeal, who can blame her for making a racket? She looked amazing; rosy and healthy. Tom cut the cord and held her and still, she screamed. The nurses took her away for all her measurements and still, she wailed. When she was finally put into my arms, I said, "Hello," and suddenly, she stopped. Instantly. It makes me cry to remember that. I haven't thought about it in so long.

After forty hours of being awake, in labor, here was my baby. The most beautiful thing I had ever seen. I never did catch up on that sleep. For the next six weeks, back at home with Marlowe, I sunk down into the mire. I was madly in love with her, but I kept thinking about what my doctor had told me: that if I'd not been in the hospital, my baby would've definitely died. I wondered if on some physiological level, I wasn't designed to be a mother. That thought, with the hormones and exhaustion, left me in a fragile state.

The focus is too often on childbirth—and not those critical weeks after. No one talks about how rough and beautiful it is. We were home with our baby and had no fucking clue what to do. It was Tom's idea to just have it be the three of us, which in moments I resented. He wanted to establish our new unit but I was really craving the company of women. Before the baby came along, I had people tell me, "Oh, those first few weeks are magic. You're in this blissful bubble," but I didn't feel that. I was breastfeeding and because she had reflux, I'd spend hours feeding her only to watch her puke it all up in minutes. I'd cry, covered in sick, while watching the Summer Olympics. The emotional shift, to being symbiotically connected to her at every minute, was harder than anything physically happening but of course, they amplify each other. There were no more uninterrupted nights of sleep. Now there were midnight calls to the midwives trying to figure out why she'd been crying for hours. They'd inevitably say, "Feed her." Guilt would wash over me for not realizing that she was hungry.

I was trying to be positive because I knew Marlowe was absorbing my feelings. If I was distressed, she was distressed. So I found myself just going through the motions with an occasional burst of bliss cutting through the numbness. There's real loneliness in feeling like you failed at the joy.

There were gestures of love that sustained me during that time. Tom cooking beautiful meals and cutting my food up to feed me while I fed her. His mother came over and tidied the whole house and it was one of the most loving things a person has ever done for me. My sister, who had a baby only eight months before, would come over and spend the night. Finally, I was getting the female support I craved.

Motherhood has shown me the necessity of knowing when to step back and detach a bit. One day, my sister and I were sitting together, babies on our laps, talking. Marlowe was only three weeks old and her cousin, who was about nine months old, accidentally hit her in the head with a remote control. I cried and Marlowe cried and my sister cried and her child cried. I felt my daughter's pain on such a deep, visceral level. **Oh fuck,** I thought, **I am screwed. I am absorbing everything she's experiencing**. It wasn't just her taking on my feelings; it went the other way too.

Autonomy has been a lesson for both of us. We've had to work to be separate people, to be connected but not codependent. It's a lesson that goes back to my family of origin. The three girls, a little team, always entwined but it wasn't always the best way. There is power in realizing that children are robust and that I didn't need to feel so much guilt for not doing everything perfectly. If you love them and are there for them—if there's food and laughter and a warm, safe place to sleep—that counts for so much.

When Marlowe turned six, our separation became more distinct. We weren't so intrinsically linked. She could be in a bad mood while I was happy and vice versa. Her independence was beautiful to witness: I wasn't peeling her off of me during school drop-off anymore; she'd skip away. Now at age ten, she's well on her way to being her own person. She's a wonderful physical comedian, joyous and strong. We share a sense of humor that is identical and there is no greater feeling than looking into the eyes of this person you co-created with tears rolling down your cheeks, laughing. It's occurred to me lately that you really only get ten years with them. The sleepovers start, the teenage years take over, and then they're out of the house. Motherhood is a life-long commitment, but the most tender years go by extremely fast.

I now understand time in a way that I never had a concept of before. Logically, I understand mortality and that there is an ending to all this. I gave birth when I was thirty so when I'm sixty, she'll be thirty and maybe will have her own children. How much time will we have together? Doing the math is this rude awakening of how precious and precarious time is. But it's also a real gift, that dose of reality. It's the ultimate root to the present moment.

Finding My Way
KATRINA YODER
Business Owner

I'd never been one of those girls who fantasized about their beautiful wedding and the name of their first baby. That just wasn't me. When I was twenty-three, I was more like, "Who am I? What am I going to do with my career?" After having a child, I still asked those questions, but with more urgency. Maybe I would've meandered more to the answers, but there's nothing like having a child to underscore how important the role of self-agency really is in building a life.

I had a sinking feeling the day I went to the doctor to, ostensibly, get my first-ever prescription for birth control. Secretly, I was worried I was pregnant. My boyfriend and I had been using the pull-out method for the last two years. I had already taken some home tests but I told myself the positive results were a fluke (twice) and threw them in the trash. At the doctor's office, the standard urine test they made me take before releasing the prescription came out positive. There was no denying it any longer. The truth was, I'd been showing symptoms for two months but I was terrified. I was only twenty-three and still in college. My boyfriend, Aaron, was only twenty-one, and not what I considered Dad material. He was hella immature and didn't know how to take care of himself yet. I had been writing off my nausea as a newfound lactose intolerance because I didn't want to face the truth.

In my car after the appointment, I broke down. I sobbed at the idea of having a baby with Aaron; I wasn't ready for any of this. But sometimes you know you need to do things, even when you're not ready. I knew that I was going to have this baby. If I needed to, I would be both Mom and Dad, like my mom had been for me. If she could raise a child on her own in her twenties, then so could I.

There's the old stereotype that a woman gets pregnant so she can trap a man. That's not how it was for me. When I told Aaron the big news, he wanted to jump right in, marriage and all. It sounds so horrible to say that I didn't want to marry the father of my child but I didn't. I didn't trust him to be reliable at all. I wanted to give a good life to my baby. I've lived in Hawaii since 1988, when I was four years old. I'm white but in many ways, I've absorbed the native culture of the island, which is distrusting of white men in particular. My baby would also be white and I was determined to raise one of the good white guys, a little feminist. I wanted to raise a good, considerate man who would use his powers to fight the injustices of the world. When I was pregnant, there were uprisings against President Hosni Mubarak's regime in Egypt. Cairo was in the news a lot as the people took to the streets. I was hoping that my son's generation would be that brave. I dreamed that he would be a part of a revolution for the people.

Being pregnant so young and unmarried made me feel a bit ashamed, as if I'd done something so scandalous. The reaction from my college teachers ran the gamut. I had designed my own degree, one that allowed me to pursue my dream of teaching yoga. Many of my classes involved movement. In my ballet class, the teacher cut me no slack, saying, "Well, I danced throughout all three of my pregnancies so you should be fine." Meanwhile, my weight lifting class was headed by a young man and everything about my pregnancy made him nervous. "You don't have to do anything," he said. "Just walk on the treadmill a bit and I'll give you an A."

Aside from the weird reactions and the tinge of shame, I actually loved being pregnant. A secret society had opened up to me. Women across all socioeconomic backgrounds were extra kind, looking me in the eye with meaning, welcoming me to the club. The sensation of someone growing inside of you is amazing and magical. I felt powerful, which is not a feeling that women in their early twenties come by easily in this world.

My experience in healthcare, on the other hand, couldn't have been more disempowering. My mom is a nurse and my stepdad is a doctor, so I grew up very trusting of Western medicine. My OB was brusque and imperious. She never explained anything to me, just told me what tests I needed done. I constantly felt belittled, and like I couldn't speak up, because she was the authority. Looking back, I wish I had asked questions, even disagreed with her. I was so young and didn't feel empowered to have that kind of dialogue with a doctor. I hope young women having babies now don't have to endure the kind of treatment I received.

When I was two weeks past my due date, my OB scheduled an induction, which was something I really didn't want. Google was rife with horror stories about women getting pumped with hormones to prompt labor. I wanted to avoid that, so I had an acupuncturist come over, and that did the trick. To my great relief, I went into labor four hours later.

At the hospital, I felt the same kind of condescension from the nurses that I had struggled with from my doctor. When they asked me to rate my pain, they didn't believe me when I told them I was at a nine. They actually laughed at me, saying, "You just started, honey, there's no way you're at a nine yet." Finally, they offered me an epidural, and I reluctantly agreed. I'd wanted an unmedicated birth, but by that point, I'd been up all night, and Aaron, who was with me, hated seeing me in all this pain.

At 6 A.M., shortly after the epidural, I wasn't dilated at all. I fell asleep for six hours, and woke up to the most incredible pressure. The baby was ready to come out, but my doctor was trapped in a meeting. I was literally crossing my legs so that this eight-pound baby wouldn't push his way out before the doctor could get there! The OB finally came in an hour later and ten minutes after that, in three pushes, baby Kairo was born. He looked exactly like Aaron's mom, which was hilariously unexpected to me. We never know how genetics will play out, do we? I loved him right away. His manner was calm and sweet, and he immediately latched. We had to keep telling the nurses that no, we didn't want him circumcised. Even after I had my baby in my arms, they just looked at how young I was and didn't trust my voice and my opinions.

Back at home, I felt like a pendulum swinging back and forth between anxiety and relief. On one hand, I had a healthy birth. A very good friend of mine had a traumatic home birth that greatly injured her child so I knew it was a blessing that Kairo came out so easily and in good health. But I still worried about him. For whatever reason, I was concerned that he'd have autism and I kept checking for the so-called signs, which look a lot like what neurotypical babies do too. But I wanted to be vigilant about everything. I was completely responsible for this tiny little baby, and I knew how important a responsibility being a mother was.

At six weeks, everything got a lot harder. I decided to go back to college because I was so close to finishing . . . or at least I **thought** I was close to finishing. Aaron and I were living together so that he could help take care of the baby. I was expecting to just bang out the rest of my credits in a summer but it ended up taking a year (and still, I wouldn't finish). I felt guilty for leaving my son all the time. It was terrible to be sitting in classes with engorged breasts. I'd race home whenever I could to feed him. I knew it was up to me to improve our situation, to provide for Kairo because I wasn't able to depend on Aaron— financially or emotionally. He didn't have a lot of practical life skills: He couldn't even make rice in the rice cooker! I'd come home exhausted from classes or teaching yoga all day and then I'd have to make dinner too.

We had two big things going for us: One, Kairo was a very easy baby. He barely cried. He slept ten hours at a time at night from a very early age, and took super-long naps. His ease charmed my in-laws into taking him for long stretches, usually overnight visits, so that we could get a break. My mom was involved too, but she didn't get along with Aaron so she wasn't as hands-on. I admit I also kept her at a distance. I didn't want her to know how hard it all was for me. I didn't want her to judge all the things I was embarrassed of: my relationship, my small and perpetually messy house, my novice parenting skills, my lack of coping skills, or my addiction to weed.

About a year or so after Kairo was born, I got pregnant again. My crappy insurance wouldn't pay for birth control, so I had to fork over thirty dollars a month out of pocket. It may not sound like a lot but it was for me at the time, and I wasn't alone. A 2017 bipartisan survey of registered voters revealed that 33 percent of women voters couldn't afford to pay more than $10 a month for prescription birth control. Factor in too that I was working, going to school, and caring for a one-year-old. Life was overwhelming enough without adding another baby to my family. I was certain I should get an abortion. The OB tried to talk me out of it. I found that so offensive. I knew that if I had another child, I would resent that child. I was already so close to my breaking point. I couldn't believe that someone else would try to make that choice for me.

At the procedure itself, a D&C under anesthesia, even the nurse hassled me before I went under. "I can't believe you're having an abortion," she said. "I've been trying so long to get pregnant." I didn't know what to say. My situation had nothing to do with hers. I was doing the most responsible thing for my family and myself. After the procedure, I recovered physically, but digging myself out from under a $4,000 medical bill was another matter. I called the insurance company in tears. "You won't pay for birth control and you won't pay for an abortion," I cried. "You've got to give me one," but they didn't care.

With one credit left in my degree, we moved from Oahu to the Big Island. Aaron was miserable; he was stuck at home all the time and made no money. I was teaching seventeen to twenty yoga classes a week just trying to make ends meet. I didn't have any time to take the final class I needed for my degree.

I hoped moving would make Aaron happy. Using my yogic values, I'd tell myself that I would have to accept him for who he was. I shouldn't try to change him. I really wanted to unconditionally love the father of my child, but after five years, we broke up. Immediately, relief flooded in. I no longer had two kids to take care of: Kairo, who was going into kindergarten, and then this man-child. With Aaron out of the picture, life got so much easier. After being in crisis mode for years, I finally had time to be with myself again. I didn't feel like a robot anymore who couldn't allow herself to feel or think about anything except what was directly in front of her. It was time to find myself again. A support system of women—friends, family, neighbors, people from my community—rose up around me. They helped in major ways, picking up Kairo from kindergarten when I was late getting out of work. By then, I was managing a yoga studio. But I knew that being a yoga teacher was never going to be enough to financially support my son. I decided to move back in with my mom and started studying massage therapy.

After our breakup, Aaron disappeared. First he chased some girl to Oahu and then he chased more girls on the mainland. While he was gone, his parents really kicked in, giving so much time and love to Kairo. Between his parents and mine, we formed a really balanced team who just loved Kairo to pieces. And that's all that really matters—that he is surrounded by people who will do anything for him. Aaron returned after a couple of years, and after a lot of conflict, we've settled on a working system as co-parents. Therapy has helped me tremendously, because all we can really control is ourselves. Aaron and I share custody fifty-fifty because Kairo is obsessed with fairness.

As Kairo has grown up, I've always made sure to raise him to be a confident and kind person. Even when he was a toddler, I spoke to him in a kind and respectful manner. I'd get down on his eye level and carefully explain why he couldn't do something. It's been incredible to see that pay off. Starting from when he was little, he'd help me when I was stressed. He knew what to say, because I'd said similar things to him. Like, if the car broke down, he'd say, "It's OK, Mom. This kind of stuff happens sometimes. Let's go wait in the shade." In those moments, I feel really proud. It's proof that I've done a good job. Now that he's fifteen, sometimes it feels like he doesn't need me as much, which breaks my heart a little. At the same time, he's still so sweet and innocent. He's still very much a kid.

I eventually got licensed as an esthetician and massage therapist. A few years ago, I opened up my own spa in Haleiwa, specializing in facials, massage, and hair removal. Things are much more stable in my life. I've found the answers to the questions I used to ask myself before Kairo was born, about who I was and what I wanted to do with my life. I'm someone who has learned to depend on herself, to be a provider, to ask for help, and to make hard choices. And the most important thing I am is Kairo's mom.

A Love That Hurts

AMY SCHUMER

Comic

I was diagnosed with hyperemesis gravidarum, a severe form of the quaint-sounding "morning sickness." Doctors are hesitant to give this diagnosis, partly because there's such a spectrum and also because there's not much research on the disease. Because, as I joke onstage, it only happens to women. Most medical research is on men. Some women can't keep any food down and they have to get a feeding tube and live in the hospital. I was able to keep food down (sometimes) and I could still gain weight, which put me on the more fortunate end. But it didn't feel like that. At six months along, I was vomiting every day, multiple times a day. It took everything in me to get onstage for an hour a night.

I would usually vomit until the moment I walked onstage and resume the second I walked off.

I had never longed to be a mom. I got my very first flash of maternal instinct at the ripe age of thirty when, at a party, I suddenly scooped up my friend's kid and no one was more surprised than me. At that point, all I wanted was an adventurous life filled with new experiences and travel, and stand-up comedy was my main vehicle for creating that existence. I got addicted to comedy; I just wanted to get better and better. For ten years while my friends were all coupling up and starting families, I wasn't available, couldn't even connect to the idea of having a baby— I was just doing show after show. Having children was truly the furthest thing from my mind. One time Barbara Walters asked me in an interview where I saw myself in five years. My answer was "directing." She was shocked I didn't say having a family. I hadn't thought of it!

Meeting Chris changed all that. I was thirty-seven, which is different than meeting somebody at twenty-seven and having years to figure out if you like each other. My family and I rented a house in Martha's Vineyard and my assistant at the time suggested hiring her brother, a James Beard Award–winning chef, for the stay. So we got to know each other around our families, which cut through a lot of nonsense right away. He saw me in a relaxed habitat with no bra, no makeup. No effort or artifice. For me, it was love at first sight. When I told him that recently, he responded, "That's nice"—not exactly returning the compliment.

My husband does not have a dishonest bone in his body, which I love. He's high functioning on the autism spectrum, and part of the way that manifests is for him to say exactly what he thinks, which was refreshing. Shortly after he moved in, I sent him a text message that said, "I don't know if I want kids. So, if that's something you want, I feel like I should be up-front about that." Did I **really** not want kids? I think I was trying to reel him in with the "I'm laid back and have an empowered, original vibe" vibe. He immediately wrote back, "I do want kids and I want them with you. And we'll have a beautiful family and it'll be great." I'll never forget reading those words, standing in my closet, jaw dropped. In that moment, I knew that he meant it. It knocked the wind out of me and I was shocked by how over-joyed I was.

We got married and started to try right away (meaning I went off birth control). After a couple of months, I was offered a role playing a boxer. Two months into serious training, I decided it wouldn't be a good time to get pregnant because I was going to be a punching bag, so the plan was to return to birth control when I got my next period and we should try again after the film wrapped. That period never arrived. I was a little late but I have endome-triosis (boooo) so it can be irregular. We didn't really think I was pregnant, but we decided to get a pregnancy test, almost for fun. In my mind there was no way I was pregnant. I had never gotten pregnant before and I assumed we would eventually need fertility help because of my endo.

I peed on the test, and then promptly forgot about it, turning my attention to important things like looking at celebrity gossip on the internet. The next time I went back to the bathroom, maybe forty minutes later, I checked it. There's no way to describe the moment. I remember wanting to be really present with it. I wanted to hold and keep forever this one minute where only I knew. Indescribable joy hit me. My heart was pounding as I slowly walked down the stairs and shouted, "Chris!" He thought I was gonna yell at him about something, so he wasn't quick to respond. My hormones must have already been rocking out because I hadn't really been a pleasure to be around. He met me at the bottom of the stairs and we stood together in the foyer. I looked straight at him and with shock I said, "I'm pregnant." We just stood there, looking at each other. Not saying anything, just existing in the moment. We were stunned and didn't fully understand what it all meant. We hugged and stood in the foyer wide eyed looking at the test for 15 minutes, reminding each other to breathe.

Once the nausea was in full effect, Chris had to really take care of me. I got pregnant seven months after we got married, so we hadn't been together that long yet. At first, it was kind of heartbreaking for someone as independent as me to be so reliant on my partner. And for him to be thrown into being an unpaid home attendant. I was too sick to get up and get myself water. Some days, I couldn't climb out of bed at all. But throughout all of this, I felt this incredible pull to work. To get things done while I still could. I think I was afraid, like many moms in the performing arts are, that having a baby meant I'd never work again. At thirty-six weeks, I flew to L.A. and pitched a show that I wrote while pregnant. I sat in a hotel room fighting back nausea, pitching my show to executives from different networks—and it worked. We sold **Life & Beth.** I shot an hour comedy special, went on a nationwide tour, and oh yeah, got arrested protesting the confirmation of Brett Kavanaugh, knowing if he was confirmed we would be on a devastating path to overturning Roe (puke). I tried not to skip a beat.

My hyperemesis got even worse at the end. I had been talked into a dreamy birth center experience upstate, midwives and pixie dust vibes, but it had to be scrapped. I was throwing up to the point where I got an IV about five times a week, instead of the standard two a week like most of my pregnancy. It was frightening how dehydrated I was. We made the decision to have the baby at a Lenox Hill Hospital, where I was born, instead, closer to home with my own doctor. Sad to leave the water birth in a meadow dream behind. But you know, you need to bring the girl back to take the baby out of said girl, as the old saying goes.

The day I was thirty-nine weeks I was the sickest of all and couldn't stop vomiting, and my gynecologist agreed to induce me. My acupuncturist and good friend Vickie Lee then encouraged me to go a step further and schedule a C-section. She said, "You've had it rough enough, and your induction is likely to end in a C-section anyway." I've had too many friends labor for days and still need a C. Vickie's words are what I needed to hear in order to give myself permission. There is such pressure to have as "natural" a birth as possible, and then to breastfeed until the kid is fifteen. No one had been pushy about those ideas, it was all self-induced, but still, people are usually really invasive with pregnant women. Ten minutes after meeting you, they will ask how long you plan on breastfeeding, as if you want to discuss your lactation goals with the person who happens to be behind you buying a bagel.

We didn't waste any time. At 8 p.m. that night, we were in the car on the way to the hospital for the C-section. I hadn't eaten anything all day, to prepare for the surgery, and Chris decided to eat a brisket sandwich right in my face. I will never let him forget this, of course. We drove by the Met Ball as they were setting up, so I jumped out of the car and climbed the stairs, where people would be wearing

Valentino and the like, and I swanned around in my maternity sack dress and leggings, making the security guards laugh, and taking some pictures.

Going into the C-section, I kept doing what I always do when I'm nervous: making jokes. When the nurse was shaving my pubes for surgery, I said, "Can you shave it into a diamond?" Things were light enough until I got the epidural. Being numb from the waist down terrified me. The severity and danger of the moment kicked in. I asked the surgical team, "Is it normal to be scared?" They were like, "Yes, everybody's scared," giggling and empathizing with the question. I said, "Well, I'm really scared." Then I started shaking a lot, despite the warm blanket the anesthesiologist had given me. The surgeon cut me open and for a while, I was just alone, throwing up in a bowl that the nurse would tuck near my chin. At first, you are alone in there.

By the time Chris and our doula came in, the vomiting had passed but I was torn open and scared. One of the common symptoms of being on the spectrum is that it's hard to make eye contact, even with someone you love and trust. Our doula told him, "Just look at her." And he looked directly in my eyes and held me there. We stared right through each other. Nonstop, endless eye contact. Barely blinking, I flashed back to that moment where we looked at each other after I told him I was pregnant. And to the moment we first met standing in that kitchen. In this desperate hour, he showed up for me. Holding me with this eye contact as if to say, **I've got you, you are not alone.**

Half an hour later, our baby was finally born. This tiny person I couldn't have ever imagined. My doctor held him over the curtain and Chris and I burst into tears. For me, violent, ugly, well-deserved tears. We had done it. I had done it. That moment was so profound, seeing him for the first time. Gene looked like the Count from **Sesame Street** because his hair was really dark, his skin purple. He had this amplified energy right out of the womb, like he was late for an appointment.

After they detached the cord, they put Gene next to me. His cheek touched mine. For a good ten seconds, I got to focus on him and the love and connection washed over me before he was whisked away and I was left to be sewn back up. Your uterus is supposed to contract after the baby's out, but mine did not. For about two hours, I felt like there was a good chance I was going to die but no one was going to tell me. It was just taking so long, and I had no idea why. Eventually, Gene was back, and Chris was next to me. It was this beautiful moment of us being with the baby but at the same time, listening to the doctors talk to each other in hushed, worried tones. It took so long that the anesthesiologist got off his shift, and another one replaced him. I heard my doctor ask if they had something to relax my stomach muscles. They didn't. I was hyperaware of everything going on and truly believed these were my last moments alive. I told Chris, "I'm ready for this part to be over." Our incredible doula, Domino, was honest with me and told me it wasn't normal that it was taking this long. Finally they said, "Okay, you're done." It was the most immense relief. The nausea was gone and I was closed back up. My body alone after all those months of having a tenant. Afterwards, they told me it had taken so long because everything was a mess inside, from the endometriosis and my uterus not contracting as it should've because of the adenomyosis (endometriosis of the uterus). In the end, it took two hours to put Humpty Dumpty back together.

Bringing the baby home was absolutely surreal and nerve-wracking. Driving through Manhattan with this minuscule honey in the back seat, I wanted to go 5 miles an hour.

We arrived home and slept, deeply, Chris and I holding each other, sweaty and dazed, until our baby nurse woke me up to breastfeed. Breastfeeding was really difficult for me. Gene never latched. Those moments where he fought it were so intense. I felt like an awful failure. I had witnessed some friends experience the same thing and I had never judged them, but when it happened to me, it hurt. I pumped and he got the colostrum for those first couple of weeks but once I realized that I could stop pumping, I was pretty psyched. It took like a month for my milk to stop coming. It was emotional to stop, but on the whole, it's a short time in babies' lives. The proven benefits of breastfeeding versus formula are slight and he's already moved on to whole burgers. What I'm saying is, **DO YOU QUEEN!**

Now that Gene is old enough to walk, I've had enough time to completely surprise myself as a mother. I thought that I would get really overwhelmed parenting (and I do sometimes), and that I'd need to escape back into work, but I was shocked to realize I almost always want to spend time with him. Don't get it twisted. I'm glad when he goes to sleep at night, but I'm excited to see him every morning. Any mothers cursing me right now, you have a right to. We are privileged, and have enough assistance that it has made it easier for me to be the best version of myself for Gene and I'm deeply grateful.

Chris and I are different as parents, in ways that I didn't expect. Though he's a sensitive, artistic person, Chris is happy to support Gene's independence, letting him climb rocks and trees, while I'm ready to carry him around on a silk pillow inside the vehicle the pope rides in. About a year ago, I came in and Chris was drilling on the wall with Gene in a carrier on his chest. I was like, "No drilling while you're wearing the baby!" Chris said, "But I've got it on the lowest setting." I held my ground: "No drilling with Gene. Okay, glad we had this talk." Maybe because Chris isn't neurotypical, we have some challenges around communication—but we're seeing a therapist who specializes in autism, and that's really helped us sort through this new world.

I've been so encouraged by how **into it** Chris is; he's not that dad that blows in to "babysit" his kid. He's an equal partner who's involved with everything.

I never once resented the pregnancy, even during the worst of the vomiting, though it was still abstract to me when people would say, "It'll be worth it." I didn't really grasp the entirety of what that meant. Knowing what I know now, I'd sign up all over again to be that sick for ten years if it meant meeting my little baby Geeny da baby da guy (what we call him) at the end. I found out I was way more resilient than I ever thought possible—and that I could depend on Chris to be there for me in sickness, and in more sickness.

From the moment Gene was born, I became an open wound in a beautiful way. People say it's like having your heart outside your body and that's the best description I have heard about how it feels. Gene is a toddler now, but that rawness hasn't entirely gone away; you just get used to it. It's this love that's so deep it hurts. It also is the most joyful, meaningful experience in existence. What else is such euphoria that you would take not only nine months of food poisoning every single day but you'd let them slice open your FUPA? You gotta do it if you can!

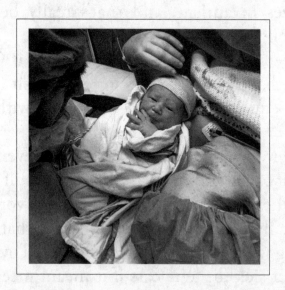

About the Contributors

LA LA ANTHONY is an actress, producer, **New York Times** bestselling author, and entrepreneur. La La is best known for her role as Lakeisha Grant on the hit show **Power,** which wrapped its sixth and final season on Starz in 2020. Anthony has since joined the cast of SHOWTIME's **The Chi,** HBO Max's **The Freak Brothers** reboot, signed on as a recurring cast member of Hulu's **Wu Tang: An American Saga,** and will join the cast of the upcoming Starz original series **Black Mafia Family.** Taking it to the silver screen, La La has also announced that she will star in the indie drama **Gypsy Moon** alongside Lena Headey and Sam Worthington, plus Netflix's **The Perfect Find** with Gabrielle Union. Behind the camera, La La will be executive producing the upcoming horror comedy for Universal Pictures,

Juju, with Issa Rae and will serve as co-executive producer with 50 Cent for two projects: the upcoming limited Starz series **The Case of Cyntoia Brown** and the new Starz drama titled **Intercepted,** based on Alexa Martin's bestselling novel and inspired by her life as an NFL wife.

Her other acting credits include **The New Edition Story** (BET) and **Unforgettable** (A&E), **Reef Break** (ABC) and **BH90210** (FOX), as well as feature films including **Think Like a Man, Think Like a Man Too,** Spike Lee's critically acclaimed **Chi-Raq, Double Play, Baggage Claim,** and Netflix's **Holiday Rush.** La La Anthony is also the host of a new Facebook Watch series titled **La La Anthony: Reclaim Your Life** and is the producer of a Snap Original docuseries titled **The Honeybeez of ASU.**

La La produced the BET documentary film **Killer Curves** and made her Broadway producing debut in 2016 with **Eclipsed,** starring Lupita Nyong'o. **Eclipsed** received a Tony Award nomination and made history as the first all-female, all-Black show on Broadway.

La La has also written two **New York Times** bestselling books, **The Love Playbook** and **The Power Playbook.** She is currently adapting **The Love Playbook** into a TV series.

She began her entertainment career in radio at the age of sixteen at Atlanta's HOT 97. Following a brief internship while still in high school, she was given her own show, the wildly popular **Future Flavas** alongside rapper/actor Ludacris. At nineteen, she received an offer to cohost **The B-Syde** at 92.3 The Beat in Los Angeles. In 2001, she joined MTV and became the network's premier talent, co-hosting the original **TRL** and **Direct Effect.**

ADRIENNE BOSH is a mother of five, wife of former NBA star and author Chris Bosh, philanthropist, activist, and dreamweaver. She is passionate about advocating for the health and well-being of mothers everywhere, and pursuing a better tomorrow for women and mothers from all walks of life. Adrienne and her husband are passionately committed to making lasting and positive impacts in their communities.

KIM DELISE is a proud native New Yorker and filmmaker, born in Brooklyn and raised in the 'burbs of Long Island. Kim is a script supervisor and a member of IATSE Local 161. She has worked on critically acclaimed projects such as **Girls** (HBO) and **The Americans** (FX). In 2018, Kim wrote, produced, and directed her first short film, **Georgica,** an adaptation of a short story by A.M. Homes. The film was warmly received on the festival circuit. In 2020, she was accepted into the Alliance of Women Directors. Kim is a '90s pop culture trivia whiz, and can tell you right now where you last left your house keys. She still calls Brooklyn home, where she can often be found on her stoop enjoying a slice of Di Fara pizza.

RACHEL FEINSTEIN is a nationally touring comedian and actress with three Comedy Central specials and numerous late-night appearances under her belt, including **The Tonight Show with Jimmy Fallon** and **Conan.** Feinstein appeared on the Steven Soderbergh Amazon series **Red Oaks** and on Judd Apatow's HBO comedy **Crashing.** She also guest-starred on Bravo's **Odd Mom Out.** Her past credits include **Trainwreck, Top Five, The Nightly Show with Larry Wilmore,** HBO's **Last Week Tonight with John Oliver,** co-hosting **The View** on multiple occasions, and several appearances on **Inside Amy Schumer.** You may also remember Feinstein co-hosting alongside Shaq on **Upload with Shaquille O'Neal.** Her latest special is part of Netflix's half-hour series **The Standups.**

Widely recognized as one of the most compelling vocalists and songwriters in her genre, LESLIE FEIST is an eleven-time Juno Award–winning solo artist and founding member of Broken Social Scene. Following the breakout success of her sophomore album **Let It Die,** the Canadian musician went on to achieve international acclaim with 2007's **The Reminder:** a gold-certified release that landed on best-of-the-year lists from outlets like Pitchfork, NPR, SPIN, and **Rolling Stone,** in addition to winning Feist the 2007 Shortlist Music Prize. Along with earning four Grammy Award nominations, **The Reminder** delivered one of the most indelible songs of the 2000s with "1234," a Billboard Hot 100–charting single that paved the way for Feist's appearance on such iconic shows as **Saturday Night Live** and **Sesame Street.** Arriving in 2011, her fourth full-length, **Metals,** was hailed as the album of the year by **New York Times** chief popular music critic Jon Pareles, and later won the 2012 Polaris Music Prize. In 2017 Feist released her most recent album, **Pleasure,** accompanied by a storytelling podcast series titled **Pleasure Studies,** which was awarded Best Podcast of the Year by Apple Music.

ANGEL GEDEN lives in the South Bay in California with her five amazing children, her supportive and wonderful partner, Mike, and her fur baby, Chance the Pupper. Born and raised in Chicago, she bleeds Cubbie Blue even after a decade in the Bay. A program manager by day, Angel strives during all moments of life to create an empathetic and inclusive space for everyone through volunteerism, engagement in her workplace resource groups, and being another human in the village of all her children's friends. A self-proclaimed introvert, Angel thinks she can make "JOMO" (Joy Of Missing Out) happen.

ASHLEY GRAHAM is an American supermodel, entrepreneur, designer, author, mother, and advocate who has been featured on the cover of **Vogue, ELLE, Harper's Bazaar, Sports Illustrated Swimsuit,** and more. Throughout her wide-ranging career, Graham has emerged as a voice for inclusivity, leveraging her platform to inspire confidence and empower others, while using her influence to transform the fashion and media industries and redefine beauty standards. She has collaborated with a variety of fashion labels to advise on and design size-inclusive collections, and is a brand ambassador for Revlon and St. Tropez. Graham currently hosts and executive produces her top-rated podcast, **Pretty Big Deal**, as well as **Fearless**, a show on the Ellen Digital Network.

EMMA HANSEN is a writer and model whose blog post about the passing of her first son, Reid, due to a true knot in his umbilical cord, went viral in 2015. Today, Hansen is trained as a full-spectrum doula and resides in Vancouver, Canada. She respectfully acknowledges and honors that she lives and works on the traditional, ancestral, and unceded territory of the Squamish, Tsleil-Waututh, and Musqueam peoples. Hansen is the author of the bestselling book **Still: A Memoir of Love, Loss, and Motherhood.**

JENNIE JEDDRY is a deeply proud parent of two, a partner, and a professional camera operator in the International Cinematographers Guild. She loves to cook, ride her Surly road bike to work, take pictures, and have dance parties in the living room. She hopes to get back to travel camping soon with her wife, Kim, and her beautiful kids, Émile and Marcel. Jennie lives in New York City, and probably always will.

ABBY G. LOPEZ, a native New Yorker of Puerto Rican descent, is the owner of Soulful Wellness Therapeutic Massage in New York City. Ms. Lopez is a New York

State licensed massage therapist, certified doula, and registered yoga teacher specializing in prenatal, postpartum, and therapeutic massage.

Ms. Lopez completed her massage therapy training at the Swedish Institute College of Health Sciences in 2002 and soon after attained her certification in prenatal and postpartum massage.

She began working in various luxury spas throughout New York City where prenatal clients often encouraged her to become a doula. Her passion for rehabilitative therapy prompted her to seek further education in therapeutic massage modalities.

In 2006, Ms. Lopez relocated to South Florida and earned certifications in various modalities while being employed as the staff massage therapist at Nova Southeastern University Osteopathic Sports Medicine Clinic, Fort Lauderdale. Here she further developed her skills in therapeutic massage assisting doctors of osteopathic medicine and physical therapists in rehabilitative treatments. Before returning to New York, she had the opportunity to work as a spa therapist in Canyon Ranch Miami Beach, The Setai in Miami Beach, and the Fisher Island Club in Fisher Island, Florida, providing massage, bodywork, and aesthetic treatments.

After completing her bachelor of arts in business management at Nova Southeastern University, Ms. Lopez returned to New York City to work in Soho House New York as a massage therapist. There she worked with a prenatal client base that quickly recognized her talent and requests came in for her to assist in labor. These experiences prompted her to become a doula.

Through her training at Ancient Song Doula Services in Brooklyn, she became more acutely aware of the injustices women of color suffer at the hands of a broken medical system. Her passion is to empower women during one of the most sacred times of their lives to ensure that their voices are being heard and respected.

In 2021 Ms. Lopez established Soulful Wellness Therapeutic Massage PLLC in New York City, where she is a practicing massage therapist, doula, and yoga instructor.

SIENNA MILLER was born in New York City, but was raised in London, United Kingdom. She has portrayed socialite Edie Sedgwick in **Factory Girl**, author Caitlin Macnamara in **The Edge of Love**, and actress Tippi Hedren in the television film **The Girl**, for which she was nominated for a BAFTA Television Award and Golden Globe Award. She has also starred in the films **Foxcatcher, American Sniper, Mississippi Grind, The Lost City of Z**, and **21 Bridges**, as well as the miniseries **The Loudest Voice**. She lives in New York with her daughter, Marlowe.

ALYSIA MONTAÑO grew up running the streets, parks, and tracks in and around Los Angeles. Her fleet feet landed her at the University of California, Berkeley, where she proudly represented the Bears as a star middle-distance runner on the track-and-field team, going on to win six outdoor championships between 2007 and 2015. Alysia took bronze in the 800 meters at the 2010 IAAF World Indoor Championships and picked up another international medal in the 4 × 400 meter relay at the Pan American Games in 2015. She competed for Team USA at the Olympic Games in 2012, finishing fifth in a field riddled with doping allegations that ultimately led to lifetime bans for two of her competitors. Most recently, she has actively campaigned for changes at the federation level to better address doping in track and field. And having experienced firsthand the challenges that accompany being a professional athlete and starting a family, Alysia has also been an advocate for female athletes to have the financial support needed to compete at the highest level while enjoying a full, healthy life. Today, Alysia is a working athlete and mom, championing the #DreamMaternity movement together with her partners at Cadenshae, Nuun Hydration, Altra Running, and United with Earth, to raise awareness and action that allows a woman to wholeheartedly pursue who she is, both as a career-minded woman and as a mother. Alysia lives and trains with her husband, Louis, in Berkeley, California.

EMILY OSTER is a professor of economics at Brown University. She holds a PhD in economics from Harvard. Prior to being at Brown, she was on the faculty at the University of Chicago Booth School. Oster's academic work focuses on health economics and statistical methods. She is interested in understanding why consumers do not always make "rational" health choices—why do people not eat a fully healthy diet, or pursue all recommended preventative health behaviors? Her work also concerns methods for learning causal effects from observational data. In addition to her academic work, Oster has written two books. **Expecting Better** analyzes the data behind many common pregnancy rules, and aims to improve decision-making for pregnant women. **Cribsheet** does the same for early childhood—what does the evidence really say on breast-feeding, co-sleeping, or potty training? Oster lives in Providence, Rhode Island, with her husband (also an economist) and two children.

AMY SCHUMER is one of the most influential figures in the entertainment industry as a stand-up comedian, actress, writer, producer, and director. She is the recipient of a Peabody Award, a Critics Choice Television Award, and two Primetime Emmy Awards. She was raised in New York City and Long Island and is a mother.

JILL SCOTT touches lives, inspires free souls and love making. She's got a bunch of awards, sold millions of albums, acts her ass off, and lives to write. She's a phi-lanthropist too. Her kid is almost a teenager. He's funny, thoughtful, smart, gifted with animals, super musical, a fly dresser, and is primarily dope af. ❤

SHILPA SHAH spent the first part of her career design-ing web and mobile interfaces for Fortune 500 compa-

nies. Although she was passionate about design, it wasn't until she was pregnant with her first son that she felt empowered to do even more in her life. Shilpa decided to apply to business school at thirty-two while having a one-and-a-half-year-old at home. Good thing she did, because through the process, she met her co-founder, Karla, and they were inspired to create an affordable luxury direct-to-consumer brand. In 2011, Shilpa and Karla co-founded Cuyana, a pioneering fashion brand in the changing e-commerce and retail spaces. Cuyana successfully marries luxury-level branding with premium-quality apparel and accessories, offering "fewer, better things" to women at accessible price points.

AMBER TAMBLYN is an author, actor, and director. She's been nominated for an Emmy, Golden Globe, and Independent Spirit Award for her work in television and film, including **House M.D., The Sisterhood of the Traveling Pants,** and most recently, the television series **Y: The Last Man** on FX. She is the author of seven books, including the critically acclaimed novel **Any Man** and the nonfiction collection of essays **Era of Ignition.** She's a contributing writer for **The New York Times** and the co-writer and director of the feature film **Paint It Black,** based on the novel by Janet Fitch. She lives in New York.

Named one of Oprah Winfrey's Super Soul 100, LATHAM THOMAS is the founder of Mama Glow, a

global maternal health and education brand serving birthing people along the childbearing continuum. Mama Glow supports birthing families during the fertility period, pregnancy, birth, as well as during postpartum, offering hand-holding through their bespoke doula services. Their doula education platform empowers birth workers around the world. Latham is a fierce advocate for birth equity and works to bridge policy gaps in maternal health. She's co-founder of The Continuum Conference, a gathering centering the experience of fertility, pregnancy, and new motherhood, as well as the Mama Glow Foundation, which advances reproductive justice through education, advocacy, and the arts.

Cultivating her wellness practice over nearly a decade, Latham has served as a doula and lifestyle guru for celebrity clients including Alicia Keys, Anne Hathaway, Ashley Graham, Karlie Kloss, DJ Khaled, Rebecca Minkoff, and more. She has been featured in **The New York Times**, **The Washington Post**, **NPR, Vogue, The Breakfast Club, Fast Company, WSJ. Magazine, Forbes, SELF, Essence,** and more. She is the proud mother of eighteen-year-old DJ prodigy, producer, and entrepreneur DJ Fulano. Latham is a graduate of Columbia University and author of two bestselling books: **Own Your Glow: A Soulful Guide to Luminous Living and Crowning the Queen Within** and **Mama Glow: A Hip Guide to Your Fabulous Abundant Pregnancy.**

CHRISTY TURLINGTON BURNS is the founder and CEO of Every Mother Counts. Christy's work in maternal health began after experiencing a childbirth related complication in 2003—an experience that would later inspire her to direct and produce the documentary feature film **No Woman, No Cry**, about the challenges women face throughout pregnancy and childbirth around the world. Under Christy's leadership, Every Mother Counts has invested more than $20 million in programs in Africa, Latin America, South Asia, and the United States, focused on making pregnancy and childbirth safe, respectful, and equitable for every mother, everywhere. Before founding EMC, Christy received international acclaim as a model representing the world's biggest fashion and beauty brands, which she leveraged to become a health and wellness advocate. She has authored a book about yoga, **Living Yoga: Creating A Life Practice** (Hyperion 2002), and has been featured on thousands of magazine covers. Turlington Burns has been one of **Time**'s 100 Most Influential People and one of **Glamour** magazine's Women of the Year. Christy graduated cum laude from NYU's Gallatin School of Individualized Study and studied public health at Columbia University's Mailman School of Public Health. She currently serves on the Yale School of Nursing Dean's Leadership Council and the Smithsonian Institution's American Women's History Initiative (AWHI) National Advisory Committee.

AMANDA WILLIAMS, MD, MPH, was born and raised in Washington, D.C. She received her undergraduate degree from Harvard University in Cambridge, Massachusetts. She subsequently moved to Atlanta, Georgia, where she received both her medical degree and master's degree in public health from Emory University. She moved to California for her internship and residency in obstetrics and gynecology at the University of California, San Francisco Medical Center, which she completed in 2005. She continues to practice OB-GYN and develop maternity health policy and programming in the San Francisco Bay Area. While she enjoys all aspects of obstetrics and gynecology, she is particularly interested in maternity care excellence, family planning, and shrinking health outcome disparities for women of color.

SERENA WILLIAMS is widely regarded as one of the greatest tennis players of all time. She has overcome insurmountable odds to win twenty-three career Grand Slams. Her remarkable tennis achievements combined with her off-court success in film, television, fashion, and philanthropy make her one of the most recognizable global icons.

Serena has won the most Grand Slam singles titles in history, with her most recent win at the 2017 Australian Open. In the summer of 2016, Serena won the Wimbledon Championships in both singles and doubles alongside her sister Venus. Overall, Serena has twenty-three Grand Slam singles titles and fourteen Grand Slam doubles titles. She is a dedicated philanthropist. She started the Serena Williams Fund, is a global Goodwill Ambassador for UNICEF, and in the fall of 2016, she joined philanthropic forces with her sister Venus to establish the Williams Sister Fund, where they launched their first endeavor in their hometown of Compton: the Yetunde Price Resource Center. The resource center conducts community asset inventory and develops a comprehensive resource network. In February 2016, Serena partnered with the Helping Hands Jamaica Foundation to build a school in Jamaica and has funded and opened two schools in Africa that are currently in operation.

Serena splits her time between Palm Beach, Florida, and Los Angeles, California, with her husband, Alexis Ohanian, and her daughter.

SHEA WILLIAMS is a passionate advocate for a clean, just, and verdant world for all mothers and families. She is the proprietor of a small photography business as well as a senior director with Beautycounter, a clean beauty brand. Shea resides in Akron, Ohio, with her husband, where they lovingly raise their blended family of six.

KATRINA YODER is the owner of Paradise Sugar Spa with multiple locations on Oahu. She is proud of the space she has created to help women feel like the Queens they are. She is passionate about self-care and practices what she preaches. Katrina believes you are a better mom when your cup is full, so go ahead and preschedule your monthly massage and facial.

Contributor Credits

Photo Credits

Page 28: David Lopez

Page 41: Katie Jacobs

Page 50: Melissa Schmidt

Page 63: The Burns Family

Page 72: Jesse Shapiro

Page 82: Julie Christine Photography

Page 107: Amanda Williams

Page 117: Michael Watford, sodaandcookies.com

Page 127: April Belle Photos

Page 152: Shane McLean

Page 162: Justin Ervin

Page 180: (left) Photo taken by their doula, Michele Arrieta; (right) Jennie Jeddry

Page 200: Rachael Brady, Branch + Vine

Page 210: Photo by Cass Bird

Page 232: Chris Fischer